"*The frameworks and ideas in this book are great ... but what I really want to say is that Gregory Gray cares, with a capital 'C.' Greg is driven by purpose, and his purpose is to help the business owners that he works with to grow and to really live! Greg and I, as fellow coaches, chat often, and we chat more often about how to really help our clients than we do how to grow our businesses. You matter to Greg. Greg wrote this book to serve, and you should read it and then read it again.*"

—WAYNE HERRING
coach and consultant, Herring Coach and Business Builder Camp

"*Business Owner Freedom is something that we thought we had. We were growing, hiring at a record pace, and turning profits, but, my, we were doing everything ourselves. Since working with Greg, he has transformed our business and taken our company to new heights. We thought we could work on our business instead of in our business, but we weren't. Then we found Greg! Greg is a great leader who has extensive business knowledge with a proven track record who can take your business to a level you haven't envisioned, no matter the industry. Greg has the perfect leadership insights on how to establish the foundation for your vision; he holds you accountable while you build the processes and guides your focus to execute the vision every day!*"

—DAVY CLAY, RYAN DELETTRE, AND JOSH SMITH
owners, Dental ClaimSupport

"The wisdom Gregory Gray shares with us in Business Owner Freedom *will bring clarity to your business vision and profits to your bottom line!"*

—STEPHEN C. DUFFLEY
president, Duffley Development Corp.

"It's rare to find business owners who are living their 'best life,' and even less common to find someone like Greg who is willing to share. In Business Owner Freedom, *Greg provides a blueprint to building a business that allows you to live a life of significance. This is one you will want to study, put into practice, and share with others."*

—BRIAN K. MCRAE
senior vice president, Central Bank Mortgage; founder, Mastermind St. Louis

"I've been working with Greg for over a year, and he is by far the best coach I've had. His business and life wisdom are at a depth you rarely see, but even rarer is his ability to communicate that wisdom in ways I can easily understand. He is constantly challenging me to change my thinking so that I can move to the next level. At this point, I consider Greg more of a friend who will tell me the truth than a coach, and I plan to continue to work with him well into the future."

—AARON WYSSMAN
owner, Ozarks Remodeling and Design

"Greg's no-nonsense approach with our executive team has made a pivotal impact as it relates to our restructuring and growth as an organization. It didn't take long to realize that we had made the right decision after initiating our engagement with Gray Solutions!"

—ZACHARY KEYTON

VP of operations, Modern Door

"I think any business owner feeling overwhelmed should read this book immediately. It's enjoyable to read and has clear action-able steps. Attention, business owners: Put an end to the insanity! There is a smarter way, and it starts with Business Owner Freedom!*"*

—DAVID KINCADE

president, Alberta Business Grants Ltd.

"Coach Gregory Gray is one of the best, and over the years Greg has helped me create the business and lifestyle of my dreams. Now his wisdom is available to you in this practical and accessible book, Business Owner Freedom: Transform Your Business to Create the Lifestyle You Desire. *"*

—DANIEL BAUER

chief ruckus maker and president of executive operation designs, Better Leaders Better Schools

"In our community, Greg is synonymous with wisdom, insight, and generosity. His candor and transparency at once draw you in with interest about his experiences and also reveal insights about your own situation that have application immediately. Greg is someone you want on your team in one way or another—as a coach, an advisor, a mentor, a friend, a neighbor, and of course on your bookshelf. In a word, Greg's views on life and business situations are 'timeless.'"

—FRANK ABLESON
president, Navitend

"Following an exponential growth period, our business came to face three 'life-threatening' challenges: the overwhelming complexity of our operations, the appearance of strong new competitors, and our loss of confidence that we had the skills to get through this. With expert guidance and insight from Gregory Gray, we gained invaluable clarity about our future path, a practical and realistic plan to correct our shortcomings, and a newfound optimism that brought back joy to our workdays."

—ROBYN AND GYULA SOOS
Dr. Soos Pediatrics of Dublin, Georgia

"Gregory Gray has a God-given intuition that has allowed him to see straight into the strengths and weaknesses of our business. His keen insight has pinpointed areas we are now working to improve, and the processes he has encouraged us to implement have set our company on an exciting trajectory. Greg coaches with courage and a boldness that is refreshing. We are blessed to have found Greg!"

—BRAD ELLIS AND R. ALLEN LINDSEY
principal, senior partner, and vice president, Flow Construction

"Greg is a rare coach who says what must be said in a way that you need to hear it, all wrapped up in a package you will appreciate. If you are a small business owner who wants genuine freedom and you want to live out your business on purpose, digest this book and implement!"

—SCOTT BEEBE
founder, Business On Purpose

"Greg knows big business and loves people and small businesses. He has the experience, knowledge, and teacher's heart to take you and transform your business. In a mastermind, he gives me treasures that grow my business and my mind-set. Whatever the size of your business and your goals, he will exceed your expectations."

—BRIAN SEIM
digital strategist and software entrepreneur

Business Owner
FREEDOM

Business Owner
FREEDOM

TRANSFORM YOUR BUSINESS TO CREATE
THE LIFESTYLE YOU DESIRE

GREGORY GRAY

Published by Advantage, Charleston, South Carolina.
Member of Advantage Media Group.

ADVANTAGE is a registered trademark, and the Advantage colophon is a trademark of Advantage Media Group, Inc.

Printed in the United States of America.

10 9 8 7 6 5 4 3 2 1

ISBN: 978-1-59932-480-7
LCCN: 2019915682

Book design by Wesley Strickland.

This publication is designed to provide accurate and authoritative information in regard to the subject matter covered. It is sold with the understanding that the publisher is not engaged in rendering legal, accounting, or other professional services. If legal advice or other expert assistance is required, the services of a competent professional person should be sought.

Advantage Media Group is proud to be a part of the Tree Neutral® program. Tree Neutral offsets the number of trees consumed in the production and printing of this book by taking proactive steps such as planting trees in direct proportion to the number of trees used to print books. To learn more about Tree Neutral, please visit **www.treeneutral.com**.

Advantage Media Group is a publisher of business, self-improvement, and professional development books and online learning. We help entrepreneurs, business leaders, and professionals share their Stories, Passion, and Knowledge to help others Learn & Grow. Do you have a manuscript or book idea that you would like us to consider for publishing? Please visit **advantagefamily.com** or call **1.866.775.1696**.

To my Father, who lives in unapproachable light.
Who created me, saved me, and guides me. To His glory
and honor, I give all that I am, do, and have.

To my late dad, Dewey Jackson Gray, who taught me and inspires me.
To my wife, Kim, whom I love deeply. Your support is extraordinary.
To my mentors in life, who helped shape my mind and path.
To my clients, who have placed their trust in me as their guide.
You are the heroes.

A NOTE TO THE READER

THE PATH TO FREEDOM

My passion for helping business owners eliminate the overwhelm that usually accompanies building and growing a successful business drew its spark from my own experiences. During my career I have encountered and witnessed others' exposure to a variety of business structures, methods of management, and cultures that define a company. The small-business owner has so many distractions vying for their attention that the idea of working on the business is often challenging. They find themselves consumed with the day-to-day responsibilities. The answer to eliminating the overwhelm in owning an efficient and profitable business lies somewhere other than in the day to day.

The path to freedom is real. Many of our clients have experienced it through focusing on the key elements of what makes a small business truly successful and self-sustained. Attaining business freedom does not mean you don't have to work hard. In this journey, you and your team will absolutely need to work hard, but you will also need to work differently than you have in the past.

My own career is a testament to this journey. I owned several businesses before I found the freedom I desired. I found a business model that provided the key ingredients to the lifestyle match my family yearned for. What I do every day is also my passion, allows for an incredible income, and is supported by my skills. I could not be in a better place to fulfill my purpose in life and experience joy in God's promises.

My mission is to help you, the heroic business owner, gain the freedom you deserve and desire. As you progress along this journey of finding your freedom, you will certainly struggle with some of the ideas presented and many of your own thoughts. Mind-set and clarity are key. Additional resources are included that can help you along the way. If you need assistance, please let us know. Now let's begin your journey to freedom.

Enjoy the journey!

"The irony of commitment is that it's deeply liberating—in work, in play, in love. The act frees you from the tyranny of your internal critic, from the fear that likes to dress itself up and parade around as rational hesitation. To commit is to remove your head as the barrier to your life."

—ANNE MORRIS,
  American author

CONTENTS

SECTION III: LASTING FREEDOM
KEY COMPONENTS

FOREWORD

Do you like practical, real-life content that can help *you* achieve *your* personal and professional goals? If so, you have the right book in your hands!

In *Business Owner Freedom*, Greg Gray provides a road map to living the lifestyle you desire by building a business that provides you freedom. Many people begin a business to take control of their life—and soon discover the business controlling them. Overwhelmed, buried in chaos, and reacting, they quickly discover life—and owning a business—is *not* what they had imagined.

As a corporate executive as well as a leadership coach and advisor, Greg has gained wisdom and understanding—and is now sharing it with you. The ideas in *Business Owner Freedom* can and will help you build the business and life you dream about. His down-to-earth, transparent, and no-nonsense teaching style will enable you to understand and begin to implement the ideas.

Greg will also tell you what you need to hear. That might not provide comfort, but it can push you to become even more successful than you are today. That is exactly what a good book should do for us!

As you can see by the testimonials, Greg truly has the ability and knowledge to influence people in a most positive way. However, it will be *your* job to practice the ideas covered here. My book *QBQ! The Question Behind the Question* teaches the powerful principle of personal accountability, so I believe it is always up to the reader to put ideas into action. That's accountability! *Business Owner Freedom* is an outstanding resource, but the content will only make a difference if you *choose* to use it.

Go ahead, jump in and begin right now—read, study, and take action. It is incumbent on you, the business owner, to make change happen and build the life you have imagined!

John G. Miller
Author of *QBQ! The Question Behind the Question*
Denver, Colorado, USA
QBQ.com

ACKNOWLEDGMENTS

I am blessed and honored to be living a lifestyle of freedom. There have been so many people that have touched my life and that have taught me lessons along the way. I thank God for placing them in my life and for the lessons learned. A book, after all, is a summary of thought that has been shaped by the experiences and influences in our life. I am grateful for these people.

Kim Gray (my wife) and Brinly and Sadie (my daughters): Kim, you have stood by me, pushed me gently, and continually edited my disjointed writings. I appreciate your patience, understanding, and guidance. Without your support, love, and encouragement, this book would still be just thoughts. I am indebted to you beyond measure. To Brinly and Sadie, I thank you for allowing me the space and time to collect my thoughts into writing. Your willingness to support me is beyond your years.

Scott Beebe (my business partner, author of *Let Your Business Burn*): Scott, your friendship and partnership is providential. I appreciate your ability to focus on the complex details and make them simple. You inspired me to get this book completed through your actions and example.

Aaron Walker (my friend, founder of View from the Top): Big A, c'mon! You have been a catalyst and facilitator of good things in my life through the ISI Mastermind and through your friendship.

Thank you for the pushes and shoves at the right time. The book is done; let's go fishing!

Dan Miller, (my mentor, author of *48 Days to the Work You Love*): Dan, through your weekly podcasts, your Coaching with Excellence program, your writings, and our conversations, your wisdom and insight has had a great impact on me. Your influence has shaped me and given me strength of purpose.

John G. Miller (author of *QBQ! The Question Behind the Question*): John, thank you for your writings and influence. You influenced not only me, but also countless others to whom I have either given or recommended your book. It contains timeless principals that are needed today more than ever.

To the men of Decem Fortis (my ISI Mastermind group): This book is now complete. It is complete in part because of your support, and your willingness to love me enough to push me. I am indebted to my band of brothers as you give me strength.

To the late Zig Ziglar, who placed me on the path of personal development at a young age. He personally handed me a "round tuit" and a signed copy of *See You at the Top*. I wonder where I would be without that spark of light.

To the many writers that I have learned from along my path: It is without question that you have had a powerful influence in shaping my thoughts. I thank John G. Miller, Michael Hyatt, Hal Elrod, John Maxwell, Jack Canfield, Gary Smalley, Malcolm Gladwell, Jay Conrad Levinson, Dave Ramsey, Dan Miller, Aaron Walker, Robert Kiyosaki, Ken Blanchard, Stephen Covey, Donald Miller, Michael Gerber, Dr. Henry Cloud, Mark Victor Hansen, Robert Allen, Mike Michalowicz, Ken Davis, Patrick Lencioni, Peter Drucker, Norman Vincent Peale, Dale Carnegie, Jim Collins, Eli Goldratt, Robert

Cialdini, Napoleon Hill, Gay Hendricks, Victor Frankl, and so many others for making the world a better place through writing.

To the many mentors I had in business, such as Joe Scarlett, Dave Krebs, Tom Hart, Roger Young, Tom Allman, and so many others: I thank you for the lessons learned and the opportunities given.

To my clients, past and present: Your willingness to challenge and be challenged is the fuel for the fire that burns within me. Being involved with you as you seek a lifestyle of freedom drove me to get this work completed. I am indebted to you, the heroic business owner, for your courage, your perseverance, and your transparency. Without your actions and implementation there are no stories.

To Business Owner Freedom Podcast guests: Thank you. Our conversations have been instrumental to continued learning and shaping my thoughts, along with the audience, on many of the subjects within these chapters.

Finally, to the team at Advantage: I owe my thanks and gratitude for your willingness to deal with my starts, spurts, and stops until we got this book complete. Your team is incredible and, in the end, made a nice book out of my scribblings and random thoughts.

Introduction

CREATE THE FUTURE YOU DESIRE

Business owner: "I thought having my own business was the ultimate freedom. *What freedom?* I feel trapped. I feel alone. I feel like a failure. I am at my wits' end because all I do is survive the day. I can't seem to get any rest or relaxation, even when away from my business. My take-home pay isn't equal to the effort I am putting into this, and even if it were, I cannot sustain this pace. When my business was just me, doing something I liked and was good at, things seemed to work better. Even then, 'business' still wasn't what I expected. Now I am overwhelmed. Where do I start?"

If you have ever thought or said anything that resembles this, you are not alone. Many, if not all, business owners experience a feeling of dread and overwhelm during periods of business ownership. Perhaps you woke up this morning dreading the drive to your business. You are not sure if you can face the team. To go through the day is so draining for you. You think, *Why am I doing this? I thought this was supposed to be fun and purposeful. I thought I would have the lifestyle I always dreamed about. Where is the freedom of owning my own business?* The purpose of this guide is to help you learn the answers to these questions. In section I, we will discuss how to identify and plan for the lifestyle you desire.

So, the obvious question is, "Why am I so overwhelmed?" There are many possible reasons: your business may have grown or your role may have changed, and you may not even realize it. People problems may be dominating your time. Customer service isn't being performed the way you would do it. You are not as profitable as you expected. The business just isn't attracting customers, revenue, or growth like you anticipated it would. You are working more hours than you ever dreamed possible. The bottom line is that all businesses have three main areas that must be working properly for success: people, processes, and planning. We will address each of these in detail in section II. The results of the business—performance, profits, and purpose—come from these three key core attributes of the business.

Once the systems are in place, and the right people are in the right roles, then it is incumbent on you and your team leaders to take the company to the next level. Mind you, leadership is important in the beginning as well. The culture of a business is one of the most important responsibilities of team leaders. The focus on your business's culture must be intentional. Successful businesses are led by action-oriented leaders who recognize and embrace continuous learning and development. We will discuss this in section III, as these are the keys to lasting freedom.

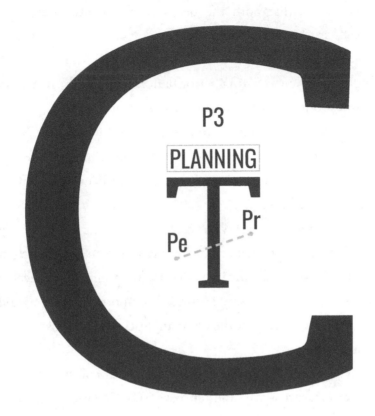

The key parts of a successful business are represented in this diagram. It starts with *Pe*, which represents people. *Pr* represents processes. They both support *P3*, or the intended results: performance, profits, and purpose. *Planning* is a critical foundation of the business as a whole. All of these elements are wrapped in the *C*, which represents company culture.

Imagine that the people and the processes are tied to each other with a rubber band. If the processes aren't in place as the people are improved, they will ultimately limit the effectiveness of your people. Conversely, if the processes are documented and improved, but the people aren't in the right roles or properly trained, the processes will not perform as they should.

The key is that both the people and the processes must be improved at the same time. Having a continuous-improvement mind-set as a business owner, and having it built into the culture of the business, is key to lasting performance. With performance comes improved profits and the realized purpose of the business.

The *culture* of the organization is critical, as it affects the *behaviors* of the organization. We will talk about that more in chapter 8. Intentionally building a great culture is necessary to drive energy into the business you are building.

Vision, mission, and values are the starting points on your journey, once we determine your life plan. As you read the chapters of this book, you will find that determining and fully developing the vision for your company is critically important. With a guiding vision, the finite energy of the company can be used most efficiently and effectively.

What is the direction you envision for your company? What are the three-year, seven-year, and ten-year strategic visions that you see as the business owner? Have you created them, and have you documented them? More important, does your team understand these visions? Are they a part of regular conversation? They should be. One last but important question about your company vision: Does it dovetail with your personal vision for life? That is a must.

Does your company have a mission statement? This is why you exist as a business. Is it clearly defined and at the top of your staff members' minds? Does it motivate you when you hear it? Does it clearly articulate your current business purpose? Can it be understood by everyone who interacts with your company? It should be an integral part of all your marketing communications (internal and external) and be reviewed in all meetings as a foundation for what actions you take and processes you put in place.

Values are also extremely important. Having three to seven key company core values will help you and your team to focus on the kind of culture you are striving to build. Some companies have more, while some have fewer. However, I have found through having worked with many companies that the ideal number is just enough to make sure all values are covered without making them complex. As these values should be clear to all in the company, fewer is better in terms of getting the message across. These values should be used as guideposts in all company decisions.

REAL-LIFE CASE

When speaking with a business owner recently, I realized that we were having the same conversation I have had many times. She was explaining that she and her team were overwhelmed, working more hours than ever, and she didn't know what else to do but work even more hours to attempt to get out of this endless trap. The company's profitability was decreasing, and they were experiencing high employee turnover—some voluntary and others involuntary. Their customer service was not up to the company's high standards, and revenue was flat. Their line of credit was maxed out, and it appeared that the company would collapse if something didn't change. "What else can I do?" the owner asked me.

My first question was why the company thought that adding more hours to the workweek was the answer to their problems. Her reply was that they just did not know what else to do. Driven entrepreneurs often fall into the trap of simply working harder. This particular company understood their business from a technical perspective, but they were struggling to understand the importance of the people, the processes, and the profit systems. They had found themselves in the paradox of working *harder* in the business to make a change

5

rather than stepping back and working *smarter* in the business to make lasting change. There is a large difference in these two perspectives: one is short-term thinking, and the other is a long-term view. We want you to have a sustainable long-term view.

It stands to reason that many business owners react to pressure this way. It seems unwise to stop doing a task that can make a difference today to focus on something that may make a difference tomorrow, even if that difference could be effective in the long term. I hear things like, "Hey, if I jump in and help, it will lower my payroll!" and "I can do that faster than my employees can, and I know it will get done."

While this may be true, no one else is in the top leadership role, and no one else is responsible for doing the things the business owner must do, such as working on the business to get the best people, processes, and planning systems in place. As the leader, this is *your* role! When you spend your time on daily tasks versus delegating them to competent employees, you are shucking your responsibility and limiting your own company. *You, at this point, are the problem.*

If you are serious about finding *freedom* in your business, read on. The steps to achieving change are here for the taking. However, keep in mind that they will require hard work, a perspective adjustment, and the realization that the process will demand consistent learning.

Many helpful resources are discussed throughout this book. You will find a comprehensive guide listing available resources in the appendix. I know that, as a reader of this book, you are serious about your lifestyle and your business. If our team can help you further, please reach out at BusinessOwnerFreedom.com. We are eager to help you and your business, as that is our purpose and joy.

"The best way to predict the future is to create it."

—Peter Drucker, American educator,
author, and management expert

SECTION I:
LIFESTYLE FREEDOM

THE BUSINESS AND YOU

Chapter 1
FINDING YOUR FIT

As an aspiring entrepreneur, I had a dream for several years of owning an insurance agency. I know most don't hear the word *insurance* and think *dream*, but my dream was about more than policies and financial plans; it was about the freedom to operate a business the way I wanted to and build my day around my business potential and goals.

While I had been running businesses for others, I envisioned the freedom—and the added meaning—that owning my own business would provide. I had a passion for life insurance, investing, and the family financial planning that goes along with this field. My close friends would often comment on my willingness to help them with their family financial planning and my deep understanding of the products and services in that field. I was the go-to guy in my circle of friends for this type of advice, and I definitely had a passion for it, so I pursued opening an agency. I was very excited about the opportunities that having the business would afford me.

As luck would have it, an agency went up for sale at an attractive price. The pro forma and financial statements clearly showed the income would provide a comfortable lifestyle for my family and me. With everything in place, I opened the agency and went to work.

A couple of years later, one of the happiest days of my life occurred. I sold the agency! I thanked God for the opportunity, the lessons learned, and the eventual sale. I could not have made a more unwise choice in a business model for myself. You see, I had the passion, I had the skills, and the income was good, but what was missing was the fit. The reality was the skills for helping others in this area didn't translate well to the reality of working in the business. When I was doing family financial planning as a hobby, as someone who helped guide others, it worked well. What didn't fit for me were the mundane details of maintaining the agency. I was trapped in the same office for five days a week, doing the same detailed work over and over, and it drove me crazy.

I can still remember the night I decided to sell. I came home from the agency that day and went straight to bed. I was frozen in the reality of being trapped by my own business. I had done this to myself. The business I pursued, the business I wanted so badly, was now the one thing I couldn't get away from fast enough. I hated it. I cried. I went through cold sweats and couldn't sleep all night. When I got out of bed in the early morning to head back to the agency, I knew what I had to do. I have never felt such relief in my life.

Whether you are thinking of starting a small business, currently own a business, or have run a business for some time, the content in this book will help you set up your business to eliminate chaos, stress, and overwhelm. It will show you how to get on the road to business freedom. The steps will allow you to create a path that is meant for you.

The first critical step is to be sure your life plan is on track. The reason to start here is simple: to successfully operate a business, it must be a part of your life plan. It must fit you in ways that have meaning and understanding. Here are a few questions that will help you decide if you are on the right path and in the right business. Take some time to answer them honestly.

FOUR CRITERIA FOR THE RIGHT BUSINESS

1. Does this business give my life meaning and purpose beyond making an income?

2. Do my personal skills and strengths fit what is required of me to be successful with this business?

3. Can this business model provide the income my family and I require or desire?

4. Does the business support my desired lifestyle?

If you answered yes to all four questions, then you are probably on the right path with the right business for you. If you answered no to any of the questions, you should take a deeper look at whether the business is going to support your life plan. Sure, you must make a living, so perhaps you can work in a business that's not meaningful for you. I have done that for periods of time in my life, and I can guarantee that one of two things will happen. Either you will leave the business because something is missing, or the business will pull you off your life's path and into a life story that is no longer yours. The end results are years of lost ambition, wasted time, and regrets. Do not become a character in someone else's story. Create your own.

You may also struggle with a lack of skills for some time; however, if you can develop the necessary skills, this too will pass. Most of the time, the skills needed are tied to your inherent strengths. If you are feeling unfulfilled in your work, then perhaps it is just not a good fit for you. The end result here is either loss of the position or a failed business. Many times, as the technician becomes the business leader, the gap in skills and strengths becomes evident. If you are running a business, there is a solution for this, which we will discuss in chapter 3.

The third question is where a lot of people start the process of deciding if the business is right for them. And, yes, income is very important. However, having the proper income without meaning and without marrying to your strengths is futile in the long run. This scenario leads to burnout, discontent, and the feeling of being trapped. Conversely, having a meaningful business that is suited to your strengths *but without profit and income* is a sure way to have a failed business. Passion cannot keep alive a business that has no income, nor can it feed your family.

I want to provide some additional clarity here. Owning a business doesn't always mean you have to work in it, at least in the long term. You can own a business and not be required to have a full understanding of all the technical aspects. Just be sure to focus on the four criteria and make certain they are not compromised, whether or not you are running the business on a day-to-day basis.

"Unless a man enters upon the vocation intended for him by nature, and best suited to his peculiar genius, he cannot succeed."

—P. T. Barnum, founder of Barnum & Bailey Circus

UNDERSTANDING THE ESSENTIALS

So how do you keep from making the same mistake I did?

First, review the questions and really challenge yourself, the business, and your life plan. If you do not have a life plan, then you are short-circuiting the process. You must know yourself and be aware of what drives you and makes you tick. Until you know that for certain, you really can't determine what business or occupation is a great fit for you. Only you can decide that in the end. With some help and guidance, you can figure this out.

The graph below illustrates a visual representation of the overlap of passion, strengths, income, and lifestyle. In the center, where the overlap occurs, is your purpose, where you will thrive. Granted, there is not only one business that will provide the answer you are seeking. There may be hundreds of businesses that will be a fit for you if they are structured correctly. If they do not fit, then you will struggle.

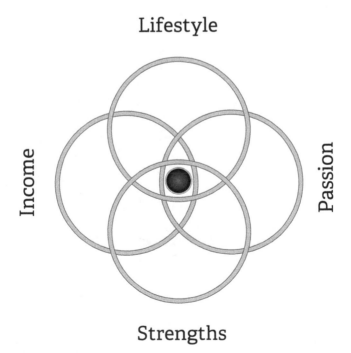

Chapter 2

DETERMINING YOUR DESIRED LIFESTYLE

Many years ago, I started an online product fulfillment company. It was a business designed to offer products via the internet that we didn't have to warehouse or inventory. I liked the idea of the potential profits that could be realized from the business model. The business also supported the lifestyle my family desired and even fit my strengths. However, I did not have passion for what I was doing. My energy waned as I attempted to get the business up and running as a side hustle. Without passion, it sputtered and eventually faded away.

In 2008, I started a direct-sales business that is still operating to this day. It is not a full-time venture; however, it does provide a good additional income. I have a team of people—some full time—who support the business. It met the criteria of all four circles and fits where they overlap. It also dovetails nicely into my business-coaching company.

My full-time business is a direct match for the overlap of all four circles. I started it in 2010, and it continues to grow and flourish because each area is supported. Through trial and error, I have become very good at making sure my business meets the criteria of all four circles on the front end of the process to save time, energy, and pain on the back end. The content, processes, and systems in this book will help you do the same. I have been through this exercise numerous times with small-business owners, entrepreneurial clients, and coaching clients. I have found there is a formula for having a successful business adventure, and it starts with *you*. You must know you!

QUESTIONS ABOUT YOU

- What is your life plan?

- What is the story you are building?

- What legacy do you want to create?

This may seem like an odd thing to encounter near the beginning a book about how to have a successful small business; however, it is the most critical step. Your answers will lay the foundation for everything else you do to build your business. Even if you are running a business of which you are not the owner, this is something you still must consider. The business you choose to work in and on affects your lifestyle. It is a major part of your story. The business and the accompanying responsibilities must be considered. You have goals and dreams for your life. The business you choose will either support those dreams and aspirations, or it will pull you away from them every day. The idea of keeping business and personal life separate sounds great in theory; however, running a business is a big part of your life and the ultimate story you are writing. In essence, it is a part of the legacy and significance you are building.

BEGINNING WITH THE END IN MIND: YOUR EULOGY

Let's create your eulogy. I have found Stephen Covey's exercise of visualizing our own eulogies, which he describes in *The 7 Habits of Highly Effective People*, to be a very effective tool for discovery. Through my experience coaching others, I have seen this as one of the most enlightening experiences to find out whom we really are. I wrote my first eulogy for myself in 2004, and I can honestly say it was an eye-opening experience. I have made dramatic changes in my life because of this exercise, and I have seen others do the same. Hopefully, you will be more in tune with *you* than I was with myself in 2004. There is only one way to find out. Let's get started.

STEP I:

To do this correctly, you'll need to find a quiet spot where you will not be interrupted for several hours. Find a place where you can think clearly and be honest with yourself. Take a clean sheet of paper and write your eulogy as if you'd died earlier today. Yes, you died this morning. It is over, and the legacy you have left is what you have done up to this point in your life.

Write your full name at the top of the page to get started. Now fill in the date of your birth, followed by the all-important dash, and then today's date. So what you have now is your name and the dates of your life. These may seem shocking or disturbing to you. Now it's time for the interesting part. Start writing what would be said about you in your eulogy. This is basically filling in the dash with the most important characteristics of your life. Be detailed and describe all the aspects of your life, such as family, career, hobbies, relationships, friends, and faith. Your words should be earnest and honest. Don't exaggerate. Just write what is reality. Thoroughly review the eulogy as if it will be delivered at your funeral. Make it real.

Once you have completed this writing, you are ready for the next step. By the way, some people become surprisingly emotional when they're writing their eulogies. I have had many clients tell me this is one of the most difficult things they have ever done. You may lament over things you haven't accomplished. You may find the direction in which your life is headed isn't where you had dreamed or planned to go. You will likely have a few regrets. The good news is these are things you can change.

There are a few questions I would like for you to answer before we go on to step 2.

1. Are there things you spend a lot of your time on that didn't make your eulogy?

2. Can you list some activities or desires that you would have liked to have been part of your eulogy but were not?

3. What are some of the things in your eulogy that you are proud of?

STEP 2:

To continue the process, you need to find a quiet spot without interruptions. This time you will be creating a eulogy ten years from today. Start with a second clean sheet of paper and write your birthday, the dash, and the date ten years from today. So now you know you will die in ten years. That does leave some time to deal with all you want to accomplish and build into your legacy. Start writing what your eulogy will say. It can and should be different from the first one you wrote. This eulogy may take a lot more time than the first one. From my experience, this one can take a full day and may even bleed into two days.

There is a lot to think about here. What changes do you want to make? What do you want to do that you haven't pursued? Who do you want to be that you have not been? These are tough questions, and the answers can and will likely change your life if you act. I have had clients call me as soon as they've finished step 2, anxious to start implementing their life plans, and they cannot wait to talk about it. People have sold businesses, started businesses, quit jobs, and even changed careers as a result of this exercise. It can be life altering, or it may simply confirm that you are on the right path. Either way, the exercise is enlightening. My suggestion is that you wait a full day, or maybe even a week, after completing step 1 before starting step 2. I've found through my experience with this process that the time gap allows for thoughts to clear from the first eulogy. As you go through the process, if you find a different time frame or process that works for you, and you would like to share it with me, please send a note to info@gregorygray.com. For additional thought-provoking questions for this exercise, go to BusinessOwnerFreedom.com/Eulogy.

STEP 3:

This step is the most critical; however, based on what I have experienced, you have probably already started the process, at least in your mind. Most people see the discrepancies between eulogy one and eulogy two very quickly. If your thoughts are similar to mine, your head may be spinning with ideas and actions to implement. I couldn't wait to get started! I wanted to change my life story and my legacy right away.

If you haven't already done so, compare the two eulogies. Create a gap analysis on a new sheet of paper by sorting ideas into three categories. The categories should be stop, start, and continue. Think through the changes you would like to make so your ten-year eulogy comes true. It doesn't mean you have to wait ten years to realize these changes. The ten-year time frame just seems to work, as it is not too short and not too long for most legacy impacts. Identify the things you want to do.

What are some bucket list items that you absolutely *must* do? What type of lifestyle do you want? Often, our eulogies contain the large impacts we make on the community or others. We write things such as loving father, devoted wife, or business owner. So the first thing you need to do is identify the most significant priorities of life and place them into your gap analysis. In the book *Living Forward*, Michael Hyatt and Daniel Harkavy refer to these as *life accounts*. Whether you call them *life accounts* or something different—I call them *life categories*—it is important to keep them focused on the biggest impacts you want to make in life.

This is your opportunity to construct a life plan that looks different than the path you are on now, should you desire to do so. Go back to the questions you answered after step 1 and reflect on the answers you constructed that dealt with your life ending at that time. Dig deep and find the most important things that were missing from your life. Also locate the nonessential activities that should be eliminated. Then identify the things that appeared in step 2 that were missing from step 1. You may even choose to think through the values you consider key in your life. These are more overarching in nature and can be like a North Star in tough times.

STEP 3 EXAMPLES

STOP	-Watching TV -Eating sugar
START	-Waking up at 4:00 a.m. -Writing a book
CONTINUE	-Serving on the board of a charity

THE POWER OF THE EULOGY

After I completed this exercise many years ago, the trajectory of my life changed dramatically. I have taken risks and stepped into uncomfortable territory many times. This is because my desire to fulfill my purpose and legacy is greater than the fear I must walk through to become whom God intended for me to be. I learned a great deal about what legacy I want to leave and what eulogy I want written and given for me. I have started businesses, stepped away from the employee world, participated in athletic events in ways I never thought possible, and stepped into the world of serving others—when I had only dreamed of doing so before. For that matter, writing this book is a result of being focused on the intentionality of my life.

I go through this exercise annually to continue adjusting my life's trajectory. However, I find now that the adjustments are very small compared to the first time I completed the process. That means I am building the right story for my life. I know I am on the correct path. I want to share with you the life values I have chosen to follow in my life and the life categories I have been using for over ten years now. I will begin with my overarching values. I've found that all of my life categories are directly related to these values in one way or another.

MY LIFE VALUES IN ORDER OF PRIORITY

1. Faith

2. Family

3. Fitness

4. Finances

5. Fun

MY LIFE CATEGORIES IN ALPHABETICAL ORDER

1. Business

2. Charity

3. Family

4. Health

5. Personal growth

6. Relationships

7. Spirituality

8. Wealth

You will notice that I have chosen to prioritize my life values but not my life categories. By prioritizing my values, I find it easier to make decisions when my categories are conflicting. For example, if I am contemplating competing in an athletic event that sounds fun and is challenging, but is also scheduled for a Sunday morning, I can easily make a decision. While I love a good race, my faith takes priority over my fun. For me, Sundays are a time to worship and praise God with other members of the church. An event that takes place on a Sunday morning sounds fun but would interrupt something that is more important to me.

The other reason I choose to prioritize my life values in this way is twofold. First, the life categories I've selected can change from year to year. My life values are stable and do not change. Second, the action plans or goals within each of my life categories can reflect different life values. For example, I could decide to ride my bike along the Natchez Trace Parkway. This is a personal goal that also fulfills my values of fitness and fun. I suggest you, too, prioritize your life values; however, your life categories can be flexible in prioritization.

PERIODIZATION

The other reason I choose not to prioritize my categories is that I often use the periodization method for completing goals. Periodization is something I learned while competing in triathlons. It is the art and science of focusing on a specific goal for a specific period of time.

A triathlon, for example, has three distinct disciplines. You swim, cycle, and run in the event. It is difficult to train for all three disciplines at once and gain a great physical advantage before the race. Throughout the preseason and the competitive year, progress is made by focusing on one discipline at a time, while maintaining the other two.

If I were to strategically decide that running is the discipline I need to focus on due to my training plan, I would devote the next eight to twelve weeks to running. While I would maintain a minimum level of swim time and cycle time during this period, my time and energy would be focused on running.

Once the running period was complete, I would switch to the next discipline. I would continue this rotation until each discipline—and therefore, my overall performance—improved. At this point, my race times likely would decrease as my physical performance increased.

Working on our life categories, we can use the same approach. We are able to work on only a certain number of things at any given time. Our physical and mental energy, our time, and our resources are finite. We must adopt a focused approach to getting things accomplished.

DOCUMENT YOUR LIFE PLAN

LIFE VALUES IN ORDER OF PRIORITY

-
-
-
-
-
-

THINGS TO CHANGE

STOP
-
-
-

START

-
-
-

CONTINUE

-
-
-

LIFE CATEGORIES IN ALPHABETICAL ORDER

-
-
-
-
-
-
-
-

VISION STORY

As you have now completed your life plan, we need to focus on where your life plan and your business intersect. Let's walk through how you create a vision story. This is the critical first step to outlining what you see your business becoming. It is important that your life plan and vision story align.

The first step to creating your vision story is to choose a time frame of three to five years to use as a focal point for the details. We have worked with many business owners, and this time frame works best.

TIME FRAME:

Describe in detail the freedom and family dynamics of your vision story. What does freedom mean to you? What does your perfect day look like? Think back to your life plan. How will you structure your business to support the lifestyle you desire?

Now think about your family. What are the nonnegotiable requirements for your time and energy for you to meet your family priorities? Do you need a flexible schedule, or perhaps days to work from home, to be there for your family? Describe what will provide you with the freedom you desire to attend to your family.

FREEDOM	FAMILY

Next, we need to outline the financials you require to support the lifestyle you have designed. Be specific in stating the following items. List the current numbers along with your future goals.

CATEGORIES	CURRENT	FUTURE
GROSS INCOME		
EXPENSES		
NET INCOME		
PROFIT		

The business may need to expand or focus to experience the growth in profit that you have projected. There are a couple of ways to do this: first, expansion can come through increasing the products and services of the business. Second, a business can experience improved profitability by eliminating underperforming products and services.

List your current and future products and services for consideration. Do not attempt to evaluate all of them right now. Just list what you can envision as possibilities.

DELETE/ADD/KEEP	CURRENT	FUTURE

As we have touched on already, a business is made up of the people who contribute to it. Let's capture what people (specifically, roles) you may need to meet the vision you have for your business. Think through what roles will be required to handle the financial growth you have projected. Again, don't try to analyze them now. Just record the best assumptions you can make at this point.

CURRENT ROLES	FUTURE ADDITIONAL ROLES

Now we need to describe your preferred customer. What does your ideal client look like? Describe that individual in detail. Be specific. List his or her age, gender, industry, and any other descriptive information so the picture would be very clear to anyone reading your notes. With whom do you want to do business?

DESCRIBE THE CUSTOMER:

One of the most important things to be able to articulate and describe in detail is the culture you desire for your business. What is the culture like today? What would you like to change? Remember, the culture shapes the behaviors exhibited within the organization. It is the personality of your business.

Be very specific in describing how the customers feel when interacting with your business. Be descriptive in the way your employees work together. How does going to work feel? Notice that we are describing a lot of feelings? That's because culture is definitely something you feel. It's the experience someone has when dealing with your business.

```
DESCRIBE THE DESIRED BUSINESS CULTURE:



```

Get the Vision Story Quick Course for free by using the code "Book" at BusinessOwnerFreedom.com/VisionStory.

THE REWARD OF DUMB GOALS

You have probably heard of "SMART goals." *SMART* stands for simple, measurable, attainable, realistic, and time based. While I have used SMART goals for over twenty years as an employee leader and business owner, I have found that for a life plan, they aren't powerful enough. They work for projects, operations, and business strategy. However, we are talking about your *life plan* here. We need to move past SMART goals and use what we call *DUMB goals*.

What you will end up with is a set of life categories that can be prioritized and connected to your life values. Regardless of your method of prioritizing them, the key is to have a prioritized plan made up of life categories. Each year, I suggest you review your life categories and create one to three action-plan items for each. The action items will guide your decisions that year to enable you to achieve your overall life story. These action items or goals need to be DUMB goals.

- **DARING**—They need to move you to the legacy you envisioned when you created your eulogy. They need to be bold and audacious. Does the goal require more than you to accomplish it? Does it require faith?

- **UNCOMFORTABLE**—Your life plan goals must move you into your uncomfortable zone. There is no growth in comfort. Does the goal make you feel uneasy and unsure?

- **MEASURED**—You must be able to measure your accomplishment. What will signal that it is complete or on track? What are the key attributes of the goal?

- **BASED ON TIME**—There must be a due date. Your effort and the goal must have a time limit, or they will flounder. Have you set a hard line for each milestone and the end date?

- **NOTE:** The reason we like the term *DUMB goals* is that many people around you may actually think you have lost your mind for believing you can accomplish so much. You will have naysayers and critics, even among those who love you. So, when they tell you your goals are dumb, you can smile and agree, because you set DUMB goals.

When you measure your daily activities based on these action items, you will see that your activities will be congruent with the legacy you are building. As you start to accomplish things that move you toward your life plan, you will become more confident and energized. I have noticed in my life as the small accomplishments begin to add up, my energy to do more increases, and my faith in the process motivates me to accomplish more.

We recommend as a periodization tool *The 12 Week Year* by Brian P. Moran and Michael Lennington. The one-page twelve-week format, which we have included in chapter 9, is excellent for managing the periodization of priorities.

Chapter 3

BUILDING A BUSINESS THAT USES YOUR STRENGTHS

*"Understanding our skills and abilities, our personality
tendencies, and our values, dreams, and passions is
the first step in identifying the right job."*

—Dan Miller, author of *48 Days to the Work You Love*

Jackson decided to become an entrepreneur. At the time, he was a well-respected engineer and employee. His employer had promoted him over the years and treated him very well. However, he was tired of the day-to-day grind that the large corporation he worked for was putting him through. The frequent travel, deadlines, and demands had become a source of contention in his personal life. He seemed to find himself often apologizing to his wife and children for having to miss yet another event. He was looking for a way out and to find the freedom owning his own business would allow.

Jackson enlisted me to guide him through the start-up plans and transition. As a result of our many conversations, he decided that the best move was to create a side business before leaving his current job. He immediately sought additional work that he could complete in the evenings and on the weekends when he wasn't traveling. Knowing this would take even more time away from his family, he talked it over with them before embarking on this journey. They were all in agreement that he should proceed. His desire was to build an engineering firm that he could operate so that it would support his desired lifestyle, life plan, and—ultimately—his legacy.

The plan was to run the side business for a few years until he could build a client base that was large enough to support his going full time. Surprisingly, the ability to go full time came sooner than he expected. Due to Jackson's reputation and engineering skills, a great amount of potential work quickly presented itself. He moved up his original time line and launched the business full time. To say the least, Jackson was apprehensive. He had only been an employee until this point. This is where having a coach can be very important. It is good to have support to move through the fear toward success, especially if the person coaching you has been there before.

With Jackson having developed his life plan and the vision for a business to support that plan, the next key ingredient of the formula was identifying his skills as a business owner.

While he had been in engineering management at his company, we came to realize that Jackson had no desire to manage employees. We looked ahead and recognized that as the company prospered and moved along the growth cycle, he would eventually end up back in a management role, which he detested. Identifying that early on kept Jackson from making the very common mistake of starting a business that one eventually hates. It's like building a new house without reviewing the floor plan and then hating it once it is built. Yes, the house may be functioning fine, but it may not suit one's specific needs. The same thing can occur if your life plan is not developed properly. It is important to build a business that supports your life plan.

Jackson ultimately decided—and his personality profile supported—that he wanted to focus on the technical aspect of the engineering business. Above all other business concerns, Jackson wanted to concentrate on maximizing the amount of technical work he could perform while increasing his income. That is exactly what he did. He enlisted several other engineers to work with him on a contract basis. Some worked part time as a side income stream, and others worked as contractors on a project basis. This suited Jackson's desire for more freedom and required no employees to manage. He could work around his family's schedule as needed and be more present in their lives. In the end, the project-based business improved his income as well. Another benefit was that he could choose to work only on the projects that appealed to him.

As Jackson's business continued to grow, he began to realize his original business vision story needed to be restructured. We decided it was time to revisit a series of important questions. The first was a simple but powerful one: "If you could design the perfect business for yourself, what would your day look like?" As Jackson considered this, I could see the light go on over his head. Now that he had a taste of life as a small-business owner, he realized the freedom that came with it also often required evaluation of how the business was doing and where it could go. He had to embrace the willingness to make a structured plan and to recognize that sometimes a plan needs to change. By honestly examining his personal goals for how he would spend his day, recognizing his own strengths and weaknesses, and committing to a business plan that would meet his personal-time requirements and financial needs, Jackson was able to experience authentic success and freedom.

Now that you understand more about the life-planning process and the vision-story process, let's dig a little deeper into the person you are. The following are some questions I asked Jackson as we progressed. I recommend that you read through them and begin thinking about yourself, your life plan, and your ideal business.

1. What are your strengths? Do you have any exceptional skills? What makes you uniquely *you*?

2. What do some of the people close to you believe are your strengths? (Ask them!)

3. What do you have experience with? In what lines of work have you succeeded in your past? Are there any themes?

4. Have there been areas you have worked in that just didn't seem like a fit for you or were a struggle? If so, which ones?

5. What legacy do you want to leave? What do you consider to be your purpose in life?

Knowing the answers to these questions is important. In the long run, it is better to stay away from things you can do but shouldn't. What that means is just because you can do something easily doesn't mean you should do it. It is true that at times you may have to do things for the business that aren't necessarily within your strengths; however, this needs to be the exception, not the rule. You must lead a business that supports your living within your strengths. This is vitally important for many reasons. Not living in your areas of strength can lead to burnout, underperformance, and even lack of success. You should focus on finding your strengths, being honest about your skills, and delegating everything else. Of course, this assumes that you have thoroughly developed a life plan and have a business that can support your legacy.

So how do you find your strengths? There are several ways to begin this process. I suggest you start with a self-assessment test. You can locate a way to obtain one in the appendix. Below is the DiSC profile that I recommend in all my coaching engagements. The DiSC profile identifies four distinct personality traits:

1. **D** — Dominance or driver: confident, direct, leader, take charge

2. **I** — Influence or expressive: outgoing, creative, optimistic, energetic

3. **S** — Steadiness or amiable: loyal, calm, listener, routine, reliable

4. **C** — Compliant or analytical: detailed, logical, deliberate, predictable

The DiSC profile is an assessment based on observable behaviors. It is the universal language of how you do what you do and why you do it. There is no right or wrong behavioral style. It is simply how you deal with challenges, people, procedures, and deadlines. It also shows how you best communicate. Learning from your profile is a great way to gather further insight about yourself.

For more information on the DiSC profile, reach out to us at info@gregorygray.com.

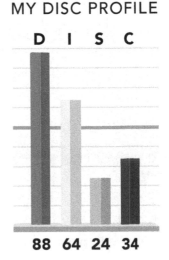

MY DISC PROFILE

D   I   S   C

88 64 24 34

Once you have completed the assessment, review your results. Did anything surprise you? What did you learn about yourself? What you learned should validate some of your answers to the questions at the beginning of this chapter. If you are currently leading a sales team and are a dominant *C*, you may find the process constantly at odds with what you are made for. However, as a *C*, you may find that accounting and detail work is attractive to you. It is vital that you find the areas that motivate you and focus on those. As an owner or operator of a business, you may think the *D* personality trait is the best for leaders. While that is a logical assumption, I have met a number of successful leaders who are dominant in the other three personality traits. What is most important is knowing who you are and making sure you are living and working in your strengths.

Another great resource is the CliftonStrengths assessment, which is focused on finding the strength themes that apply to you. Take this assessment now at https://www.gallupstrengthscenter.com. Once you gather the results, read about how to apply your strengths and grow in those areas. One key pronouncement by Tom Rath in *StrengthsFinder 2.0* is, "Our studies indicate that people who do have the opportunity to focus on their strengths every day are six times as likely to be engaged in their jobs and more than three times as likely to report having an excellent quality of life in general." These study results validate the belief that when we work in our strengths, we typically interact more with our work, enjoy it, and feel better about our life experiences overall. It is very important to understand this as a business leader; it is one of the keys to finding true freedom in your business.

For many years I lived and worked in areas that were not my strengths. I did not even recognize it at the time. I was successful in my endeavors; however, I always felt something was missing—

something was lacking in my daily existence. The stress and strain started to wear on me over the years. I started moving from job to job and wasn't sure why.

Sure, I was growing in my career, and advancement was part of it, but there was more to the inquisitive feeling. I had to understand why I was always yearning for more. And what did "more" even mean? I wasn't sure. I didn't get my first glimmer of insight until I became the general manager for a company in the manufacturing space. The position allowed me to deal with mentoring and coaching people at all levels within the organization. That was something I had not done very much of in previous roles. I had always seemed to find myself teaching others, but it was from more of a technical standpoint. I didn't see the trend until it became a part of what I had to do on a regular basis. I thoroughly enjoyed mentoring and coaching others, and I was good at it. I had found something I excelled in and was passionate about and recognized its value.

This slight turn in my life trajectory led me to learn more about myself. I realized I needed to find out what natural strengths, desires, and potential skills I had within me. I took many personality assessments, such as the Myers-Briggs Type Indicator, the DiSC profile, the Predictive Index, and others. I found things like CliftonStrengths to be of great value as well. The bottom line is, through assessments, asking others' opinions, reading books by thought leaders, and seeking out coaching, I began to know myself. Now I could seek to create a life plan that allowed me to be truly successful and purposeful. I wanted to seek significance along with success. I am on that path now and have never been happier or more aligned with my purpose.

"There are two kinds of success. One is the very rare kind that comes to the man who has the power to do what no one else has the power to do. That is genius ... But the average statesman, the average public servant, the average soldier, who wins what we call success, is not a genius. He is a man who has merely the ordinary qualities that he shares with his fellows, but who has developed those ordinary qualities to a more than ordinary degree."

—President Theodore Roosevelt

For additional information and some actions you can take if you are unsure about what you were made to do, I recommend *48 Days to the Work You Love*, by Dan Miller. In this book, he gives some great advice and exercises. These exercises are designed to help you make changes as well as identify your skills and how to best use them. If you need additional assistance and are interested in digging deeper to find out how you can transition your current business to fit your strengths and life plan, please contact us at www.GregoryGray.com.

DELEGATION—THE KEY TO GROWTH

So, what do you do if you find that some of the areas you are working in are not supported by your strengths or desires? This is common, especially for small-business owners who are growing from the technician to the owner phase of their responsibilities. The solution for this is developing roles and responsibilities for these areas and creating a delegation plan. There are many things you must do when you are starting out as a business owner that should be delegated to another member of the team as soon as possible. You need to list all the things you are doing and categorize them in one of three ways:

1. It gives me energy; it is a skill of mine, and I should do it.

2. It doesn't drain my energy, and I do it well, but someone else can do it.

3. It drains my energy, regardless of whether I'm good at it. Someone else should do it.

EXAMPLE LISTING

RESPONSIBILITY	CATEGORY	DELEGATE TO	DATE
CREATING INVOICES	2	BOOKKEEPER	JUNE 7
EDITING PODCAST	3	VIRTUAL ASSISTANT	TODAY
MAKING SALES CALLS	1	N/A	N/A

For items in category 1, which should be the chosen few, you will keep these as your core responsibilities for now as the business owner. These are things you look forward to doing, enjoy doing, and are excellent at accomplishing. They give you energy. However, you may still delegate some of them in the future as the business grows. Remember this is dynamic and can always change as the business changes.

Items in category 2 are things that aren't draining your energy, but they can be taking your time away from other more important activities. They are things that you may be good at, but someone else should take care of them so you can focus on the category 1 items.

The items in category 3 need to be delegated as soon as possible. These are things that drain your energy. Even if you are competent at doing these activities, someone who is energized by doing them will do a better job and enjoy them. Focus on getting these delegated immediately.

> TIP—IF YOU WANT TO SUPERCHARGE YOUR EMPLOYEES OR THOSE WHO WORK WITH YOU, HELP THEM FIND THEIR STRENGTHS.

"The skills that get you to the first level are not the skills that will work at the next level."

—Gregory Gray, founder and CEO of Gray Solutions, LLC

In 2010, Marcus decided he wanted to start a business. He didn't know what business he wanted to start, but he knew that he wanted to take control of his financial future. He wanted to build equity in his own company that would also have long-term positive financial results. When we spoke with him, Marcus also expressed the desire to eventually quit his job and work in the business full time. We constructed his life plan and determined how this business would fit into his life story.

Through a business-match interview process, which is a series of questions that we took him through, and the vision-story process, we determined he should look for something in the service industry, specifically in the franchise arena. Marcus, while a very bright individual with great sales skills, did not have the business acumen to start a business from scratch in an unknown industry. The franchise concept would allow him to lean on the franchisor for rapidly learning systems and processes that are vital to be successful. We also determined that he would keep his current job for the time being, and his wife and business partner, Lisa, would conceivably run the business.

Lisa also had limited experience in running a business. For many years she had worked as a sole proprietor in real estate, but she had not gathered experience in managing people and building business systems. She was a people person and possessed a strong work ethic. With the backing of the franchise systems, it seemed plausible that her role would be to lead the company in the start-up stage. However, once the company grew past the first stage, a recruiting search would begin to find a general manager who could lead the business to the next level. We created a vision story and a three-year business plan based on these concepts.

As Marcus and Lisa are continuous learners, they quickly gathered the knowledge they needed to get the business up and running. They hired their first employees, and they developed policies and procedures based on the franchise concepts. Lisa learned everything she could about the technical aspects of the business. She learned how to relate to the customers, and the revenue grew. The business was launched successfully. Through the first year, they had much to learn, such as financial reporting, sales, marketing, employee management, payroll, and leadership. The first year was literally as much an education for them as it was running a business. We walked through each of the factors of a scalable and growth-oriented business during the business-choice process and throughout the first year. The business they chose and the way we constructed it within the franchise model clearly satisfied each of these. The areas we had to work on the most were in attracting and hiring the right people and building a high-performance culture.

Chapter 4

LIVE LONG, SCALE YOUR BUSINESS, AND PROSPER

It is very important that your business and you as an individual must both prosper and grow. The truth is that your business will only grow to the point that you allow and can support.

"People cannot give to others what they themselves do not possess."

—John C. Maxwell, American author, speaker, and pastor

If you discover your business has stagnated, it generally means that you are holding it back. Whatever your business, whether you are the business leader or business owner, it must have the ability to scale. At least it must be able to grow to the point that it supports you financially and meets the legacy you choose. It must support the life plan you outlined. With business growth, the lifestyle business can become more than just another *J. O. B.*

Factors that identify a scalable or growth-oriented small business include the following:

1. A defined target market and an avatar that clearly represents your ideal customer

2. The industry or niche that supports an emerging market

3. A solid business model, processes, and systems

4. The right people and the ability to attract the right people

5. A high-performance culture and team trust

6. A clearly defined business plan and strategy

7. Profits

We will discuss each of these factors at a much deeper level in sections II and III. For now, understand that these factors are real, and each has a great impact on the growth potential of your business. You, as the business leader, must be diligent and intentional in addressing each one of these factors. Failing to address or completely understand any one of them can substantially impair the growth of the company.

Factors that identify a growth-oriented high-performance business leader include the following:

1. Has a desire for continuous learning and application

2. Has the ability and skills to delegate

3. Lets go and focuses on his or her own strengths

4. Can hand off responsibility and yet own the proper level of accountability

5. Works *on* the business and not just *in* the business or has identified and hired someone who can

LEADERSHIP

For those who are business owners, this subject can be somewhat confusing. Often, owners believe they must be the leader. In some sense, they do have to lead. They do have to make decisions for the business from an overall strategic perspective. They must be involved in the strategy, growth, and direction. However, they can recruit and hire someone with the right skill set to be the day-to-day leader, should they need to do so. We have helped many clients find the right person to lead and manage the day-to-day business.

As the person who starts a small business, you are more than likely referred to as the *technician.* You are the person who understands the specific technical skills of the business that allow you to perform the functions to meet your customers' needs. Many times, technicians start a business to escape a job or to increase their own income. Others do so because they want to create a better, more efficient way to do things. Regardless of the reason, a person with technical skills can have a very successful, growth-oriented business. However, you must develop the skills to become the leader the business needs or find someone who can fulfill that role. Either way, it is important for you to thoroughly understand each of the factors that a growth-oriented leader must possess.

All growth-oriented business leaders, as well as high-performing leaders, exhibit the desire for continuous learning. The only way to develop skills and grow personally and professionally is to seek education and then implement what is learned. Whether the thirst for knowledge is satisfied through mediums such as books, seminars, mentors, coaches, masterminds, or podcasts, the knowledge itself must be applied. Knowledge without application is only trivia! Wisdom is applied knowledge.

Delegation is a very important skill to master. The effectiveness and efficiency of delegation can be a key factor in the correct actions being accomplished in a timely manner. Improper delegation tactics create mistrust and ineffective actions.

High-performance leaders know their own strengths and weaknesses. They are adept at focusing on their strengths because they realize they will be more efficient and effective when working in their strength zones. They also understand their areas of weakness. When needed, they will delegate work to a team member whose strengths lie within that specific area.

To grow a small business, the business owner must be able to hand off responsibility for some areas of the business to other individuals. The only way to truly leverage oneself as an owner and leader is to let others assume responsibility for areas where their strengths lie. True growth for a company is the result of the company's ability to leverage itself without putting too much stress on the structure of the company. This is accomplished by not only having strong systems and processes in place but also by managing the proper distribution of responsibility and accountability.

SOMETIMES YOU MUST LET GO TO GROW

"The best executive is the one who has sense enough to pick good men to do what he wants done, and self-restraint to keep from meddling with them while they do it."

—President Theodore Roosevelt

When Marcus and Lisa started their service business, we spent the greatest amount of our time together focusing not on the business as a whole but on the owners themselves. As they were starting a franchise with a framework of systems and processes, it was the obvious choice. For Lisa, it was imperative that she learn to build and lead a high-performance team. She had to learn to delegate while remaining accountable for the results. We worked to identify her strengths so she could capitalize on those while finding employees who had strengths in areas she did not. Even when the focus is on leadership development, certain abilities and natural strengths come into play, as do weaknesses. As the year progressed and the business grew, a very predictable thing happened: the business hit a new level. Along with that came a whole new set of challenges. Lisa called me from her office in tears one day near the end of the first year, saying she had called Marcus and quit. She went on to say that she was at a loss as to how to run a business like this one. She felt like the business had become something she didn't recognize. I told her to stay put, and I would be there within an hour.

As I drove to her office, I thought through the discussions I'd had over the past several months with Lisa and Marcus. I knew we had talked about the growth trajectory of the business and that eventually the day would come that they would need to hire an operational leader. They needed a leader who possessed the skills and experience to not only run the day-to-day operations but also to keep growing the business.

When I arrived at Lisa's office and reminded her that we had planned for this day, she appeared relieved. She simply didn't want to fail, and suddenly, she'd begun to feel trapped in something she did not like. She went on to say that she truly enjoyed the sales and marketing part of the business; however, the operational activities and management of the numerous employees they now had were becoming too much for her. We talked about her natural strengths, which we had identified over a year ago. The next step was to find a leader—a general manager—to take things to the next level. Lisa had to let go to grow.

Marcus and Lisa embarked upon their business venture with clear expectations and a plan, and the two of them put in a lot of hard work. This is why their business has become a success. They made the correct hire, Rodney, for the general manager (GM) position and transferred responsibility and accountability to him. Several years have passed since then, and they haven't regretted their decision for one minute.

It is tough to let go, have faith and trust, and pay someone a significant amount of money to run your business. However, it can be one of the most financially and mentally rewarding decisions. In the case of Lisa and Marcus, it was the only thing that allowed them to substantially grow their business while maintaining the lifestyle they desired. By the way, Lisa assumed the sales and marketing role for the business, and she is as happy as ever. Of course, Lisa and Marcus are still the business owners and review the key metrics and profit and loss (P&L) with Rodney each month to provide oversight.

THE LEADERSHIP TEAM

One of the crucial steps in creating a high-performance culture in your business is the establishment of a leadership team. When your business reaches a certain size, the best way to push responsibility down into the organization and delegate the daily leadership responsibilities is through the members of the leadership team.

The team should be made up of the functional managers who oversee different areas of the business. Their roles and responsibilities documents should detail their duties in each of these areas. All members of the leadership team should be expected to come prepared to discuss the results of their efforts and the future needs within each division.

The team should meet once a week for an hour to review the performance of the organization and the section represented by each manager. The action-item list and open projects should be reviewed for obstacles, progress, and clarity. New action items or opportunities should be brought forth as well.

The purpose of the leadership team is to facilitate momentum and actions moving forward with the strategic objectives of the organization. The "big rocks," or priorities, are important to the organization, as they are what move the dial toward the main objective of the vision story, and ultimately, the business owner's life plan.

THE VISIONARY AND THE INTEGRATOR

As your business grows and the need arises to install an operations leader, high-performance leadership becomes vitally important. The business owner and the operations manager not only need to exhibit high-performance leadership skills for the team; they also need to have an understanding of the working relationship between themselves. We recommend creating a leadership agreement that will be signed by each person. This is done separately from the contract for employment or any other hiring document. This is a one-page document clarifying the rules of engagement between the two parties. An example of the document is included below. You can download a PDF version at BusinessOwnerFreedom.com/LeadershipAgreement.

LEADERSHIP AGREEMENT

PURPOSE: The purpose of this Leadership Agreement is to clearly define the rules of engagement for the visionary and integrator relationship. Refer to the Roles and Responsibilities of each for specific job responsibilities.

RULES OF ENGAGEMENT:

1. The visionary agrees to let go to grow. The integrator agrees to remain consistent in pursuing the transition.

2. We agree to meet once a month, at a minimum, to get on the same page. We will consider this meeting a high priority and will treat it as such. We will follow meeting protocol.

3. The visionary agrees to funnel requests that go around the integrator back through the proper channel so there are no misunderstandings.

4. The integrator agrees to communicate to the visionary when he or she is being compromised.

5. We agree to mutually respect each other and to not have conversations with others within the organization about each other.

6. We agree that tension will exist, and it is proper for this relationship. It is through friction that better decisions will be made for the company.

7. We agree to speak up and clearly express our opinions.

8. We agree to listen thoroughly to the other and seek to understand his or her full opinions.

9. We agree that the integrator is responsible for the final decision on operational and tactical daily matters.

10. We agree that the visionary is responsible for the overall strategy and the longer view.

11. We agree that the integrator is responsible for driving the company culture through the vision, mission, and values.

12. We agree that the visionary is responsible for continuously supporting and exemplifying the desired company culture.

13. The visionary will bring all strategic ideas and projects to the integrator for dissemination to the action list and associated assignments.

14. On a weekly basis, the integrator will communicate to the visionary the current status of all actions and projects.

Signed,

VISIONARY: _____

INTEGRATOR: _____

We have included in this document the *visionary* and *integrator* (V&I) terminology from *Rocket Fuel,* by Gino Wickman and Mark C. Winters. The visionary in the relationship is typically the entrepreneur or business owner. The integrator is in charge of the business's operations.

The visionary is responsible for setting the strategic direction for the company. If you, as a business owner, are more operationally minded, you will still need to find someone who can assist you in establishing the company's direction. We have seen some business owners ultimately hire a CEO to take the business to the next level, because this is not their strength. As the owner, you still have the ultimate responsibility for the company's direction. Typically, however, the entrepreneur is the visionary; this is what we normally see in our engagements.

> **VISIONARY:** idea person, influencer, strategic thinker, enthusiast, deal maker, opportunist
>
> **INTEGRATOR:** implementer, communicator, mentor, leader, culture driver, skeptic

Typically, the business owner who started the business is a visionary. This isn't *always* true, but it is usually the case. So, visionary, let me speak to you candidly. Notice I used the word *let*; this is not a coincidence. Visionaries tend to have a hard time letting go. This can be due to the fact that their business is their baby—their passion—or simply that they have always made all the decisions. Some obstacles for the visionary are being unwilling to let go, attempting to do multiple jobs within the organization, occupying seats that ultimately report back to the integrator, and trying to do the duties of both the visionary and the integrator.

I have seen some business owners say they want an integrator and even pursue getting one on board, only to then derail their effectiveness by undermining them at every turn. Normally what we hear is, "They don't do it the way we've always done it!" Visionary, this is why your business isn't growing! That which got you to this level isn't capable of taking you to the next level. Let go to grow!

Integrator, you must have thick skin and a relentless pursuit of transitioning the business. Without your undying persistence, the visionary will not learn to let go. Obviously, the visionary must work on this as well, or you will find yourself looking for another job. I say this with all sincerity because there is great tension that can occur at the beginning of a partnership. It is not a journey for the frail. You must be able to speak up and share your insights.

Following are some rules that we have used very successfully in establishing a V&I relationship:

1. Have at least one meeting each month (we prefer one meeting each week) to get on the same page. This is a mandatory discussion. Follow what we teach about meetings—for example, create an agenda and take notes. Make it happen!

2. You each must support the organizational alignment that exists due to this relationship. The visionary cannot allow others to go around the integrator, from an organizational perspective. If someone comes to the visionary directly, simply ask whether that individual has spoken to the integrator about it. If not, direct him or her to do so immediately. It's that simple. If I had to pick one thing we have seen throughout our many years that most undermines the V&I relationship, this is it.

3.   When a final operational decision must be made, the integrator has the final say. Here, we are talking about operations and daily decisions, not strategy. Sure, if there is something that is out of line with the company's mission or values, the visionary should invoke what we call a veto. This should be rare and not necessary for the most part. If it is common, then the wrong person is in the integrator position.

4.   The V&I must have mutual respect and support for each other. Both roles are critically important to the success of the company. Talking about each other outside the relationship is the beginning of a downward spiral that often leads to the failure of this relationship.

5.   We assist our clients in developing a leadership agreement. We have learned that putting this agreement on paper helps to eliminate many of the issues that come from the V&I embarking on their new relationship. If you study some of the most successful companies in our nation's history, you will find a powerful V&I dynamic. Microsoft, Apple, and Disney, among others, have a V&I relationship that has fueled their success.

6.   Embrace the tension. There is supposed to be friction in this relationship! There is good tension and bad tension, however. The V&I cannot take each other's questioning personally. Each party has the right and the responsibility to ask questions of the other; it is for the betterment of the company. However, the visionary cannot use the questioning as a way to manipulate and coerce the integrator into doing exactly as he or she wants. This type of passive-

aggressive browbeating causes undue stress and lowers trust. Stick to a level of positive tension. The visionary knows that he or she will not do everything in the exact same way the integrator will. This is a good thing! I'll say it again: let go to grow.

7. The culture of the organization is critical to the establishment of the V&I relationship, the organizational trust level, and the overall success of the company. While the integrator has the responsibility of developing and driving the company culture, the visionary must support these efforts completely. We have seen the visionary sometimes derail the work of the integrator by not supporting the culture that is being developed. The visionary usually says all the right things, but when the rubber meets the road, he or she undermines it through actions. Visionary: Don't do that! You must accept the culture change and embrace it; it is for the good of the overall company. Often, visionaries don't like the processes and systems that a growing company requires. It is not how they are wired. They know what the integrator teaches them about these needs, but sometimes they don't think the needs apply to them. They do. They apply to everyone in the company.

Following are the steps we go through to get the V&I alignment started:

1. Identify the organization's V&I

2. Define the roles and responsibilities of each

3. Create a leadership agreement

4.   Establish meeting rhythm

5.   Communicate to the leadership team

6.   Review the process and progress (ongoing)

CLARITY

At this point, you should be very clear on your life plan, the vision story for your business, your strengths, and how to start building a team. To make your vision for your business become a reality—so you can fulfill your life plan—you will have to give some energy and effort to outlining some key components.

In section II, we will discuss the three key areas of your business: people, processes, and planning. Without tackling these three components, you will continue living in chaos and overwhelm. With them solidly in place, your business will work for you versus you working for your business.

THE THREE *P'S* OF SUCCESS

Chapter 5

PUMPING UP PROCESSES

The way for a leader to increase their leverage is by focusing on building strong systems and processes. The only way to do this is by intentionally working *on* the business, not *in* the business. The underlying structure of the business is a critical part of the leader's responsibility. If the business owner does not have the skill set, experience, or natural strengths in this area, they must find the appropriate person to hire or find a third party who can guide them in putting these strong systems in place. The owner must give authority and offer support to the right individual to enable them to successfully build the business structure. Typically, in a small business, this person is also the day-to-day manager and growth leader.

The definition of a process is a set of orderly activities to accomplish a specific result that usually flows across multiple systems, and, at times, other processes. Your business has many processes that are performed multiple times each day. Creating a system is a primary function of the business that must be accomplished for the business to operate as intended.

"A system is a set of things, actions, ideas, and information that interact with each other, and in so doing, alter other systems."

—Michael E. Gerber, American author

Just like the human body has eleven primary systems, a business has primary systems that must each be healthy and performing ideally so the business can operate optimally. When a primary system within the human body is not functioning well, it negatively affects the entire body. When a system within a business is weak or missing, it negatively affects the business as a whole. At a minimum, it keeps a business from working at an optimum level.

To have a culture of continuous improvement, you must first identify and explain the primary systems of the business. These must be clear and documented. In this process, you may find that some necessary systems are missing. Take decisive action and get these in place as soon as possible.

Next, the key processes need to be identified and documented. These documented processes are often called *standard operating procedures*, or *SOPs*. An SOP is important for several reasons. First, it outlines who is responsible for each step in the process. Second, it defines the steps of the process. Third, it describes how the process is measured. All of these key aspects of a properly written SOP are fundamental to successful processes. Only once the systems and processes are identified and documented can continuous and lasting improvement activities begin.

An SOP needs to be easily understood and visible to all responsible stakeholders who are performing a portion of a specific process. Without visibility and clear understanding, a process can and likely will fail at some point. The results will not be satisfactory. Unless the process is measured through key performance indicators (KPIs), it cannot be objectively known if the process is achieving the intended results. The process must be documented, visible, and understood if it is to be followed. Then it must be measured so the proper results can be confirmed. If everything is measured and visible during the process, then efficiency is realized. As portions of the process fall outside the intended results, the issue is immediately identified as needing attention. If root cause analysis and elimination are properly applied, great gains can be made.

"You can take great people highly trained and motivated, and put them in a lousy system, and the system will win every time."

—Geary Rummler, president, Rummler-Brache Group

Marcus and Lisa's business story is only getting started. The company grew during the first year as they executed their strategy. Soon the business became more complex, so they decided it was time to hire a GM to help take the company to the next level. Rodney was given the responsibility of leading the management of the day-to-day operations and preparing the business for growth. As does everyone, Rodney has his strengths and weaknesses, but he is a continuous learner and is not afraid to ask questions.

Rodney called me a year into his adventure with Marcus and Lisa and said he needed some guidance. He was concerned that things were starting to fall through the cracks in certain areas of the business. He was also concerned about the internal workings of the business from an accountability standpoint. We discussed the expectations he had of the employees and how they were being communicated and measured. We also discussed the key measurements for the business. He agreed that they had some work to do.

We set a series of monthly coaching meetings for Rodney and the team and outlined a plan to go over their current processes and review their systems. Through these meetings, we determined the current state and then outlined a future state through process mapping. As I explained to them, to continue along the growth path they desired, they needed to have a solid understanding and implementation of the correct processes and business systems.

I explained to Rodney and his team that a business process is the path that is followed to complete a set of activities. These activities lead to an eventual result. A system is an area of responsibility, which we refer to as a *department* or *function*.

Just as the human body has eleven main systems, such as the nervous or respiratory system, a business has a set of systems that are required for complete functionality. If one system is weakened, all systems can be affected. These systems can be damaged or overworked as a result of the first system's weakness.

S—Save

Y—Your

S—Self

T—Time

E—Energy

M—Money

Processes generally flow across multiple systems. We reviewed an example to help Marcus and Lisa's company understand the difference. The process they currently have for managing their inventory is simple: they ask that when removing an item from the warehouse, the staff members list the item and quantity in the inventory logbook that resides in the warehouse. At the end of the month, the controller enters the inventory usage into the accounting software. The process is the summary of the steps they take to capture inventory usage. The systems affected are accounting, inventory, and operations. It was obvious that an automated process could be devised that would be more efficient and accurate. Rodney admitted that he must stay on top of the staff members to use the log, and they struggled with accuracy.

One other key point that I discussed with Rodney and his team was that processes can be independent, but many times they are dependent on other processes. We used the inventory-control process to explain this point. I reminded them that the inventory process was linked to a finance process—so the finance process is dependent on the inventory process. Therefore, the proper newly designed automated process would interact with both the inventory process and the finance process.

Another point made was that a process is significant, but it is not one of your values. You can change a process, but you should not waver on your values. A process is critical to supporting your values, your plans, and your desired results; however, it should never sway you into changing the underlying values upon which your business was built.

There are a few key points to highlight from the example above:

First, a process is a set of activities that leads to a desired result. It can also be described as a sequence of events that enables people to do what needs to be done. Many times, it is called *workflow*. Second, a system is one of the key functions of a business. A system is about facilitating the execution of processes, and it is mostly bigger and more encompassing than one process. A definition I am partial to is the following: a system is a set of processes that can run automatically without you. Systems should speed up processes by supporting them from an accuracy, timing, and quality standpoint. Third, processes can be independent; however, it is common that they depend on other processes in the business.

A SIMPLE PROCESS

INPUT-> WORK SEQUENCES-> OUTPUT

A TYPICAL PROCESS MAP

This process map shows the responsibility swim lanes, labeled on the left. The process is diagrammed across the lanes and shows where the handoffs occur. The diamond shapes represent decision points. The rectangles are either initial inputs (red) or steps in the process (gray). The cylinders represent the gathering or storage of data. The power of the process map, or flowchart, is that it places the overall process in an easily understood visual format.

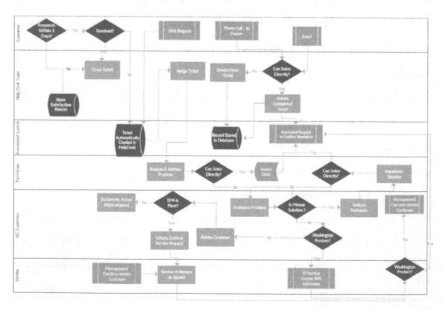

Note: The source of this process map template is www. creately.com. It is a good resource for creating your business flow-charts and many other tools used in continuous improvement and problem-solving.

Look at your current business. Where would it most benefit from clearly defined processes? If you have never experienced building a business before, and specifically outlining processes, it can appear to be a daunting task. Here are some functional systems that need to be reviewed to be sure they have solid, documented processes in place. Some of them may appear to be above and beyond what your business needs. This may be true in the beginning stages, but if you plan to grow and scale, most of them will be required at some point.

1. Sales

2. Marketing

3. Inventory

4. Human resources

5. Finance

6. Payroll

7. Legal

8. Customer service

9. IT

10. Operations

A business must have clearly defined *sales processes* from the initial prospect through the closure of the deal. Sales encompasses the activities that occur to create revenue and add value to the customer. The sales processes should be connected to marketing and customer service. Sales processes to consider are customer-relationship management (CRM), point-of-sales (POS) systems, and sales training.

Marketing encompasses the activities that identify the prospects and prepare the market for the sales processes. It is ultimately responsible for leading the way in establishing your brand. Marketing can include processes for brand management, social engagement, education, and prospect exposure, among other things. This is different than sales and should be a support to the sales processes. Tools and systems used for marketing are social media marketing, auto responders, press releases, direct mail, call centers, and traditional media, among others.

An *inventory* tracking system and processes are important for businesses that have physical products that are consumed or sold. It is important to keep track of items that are critical to the business and that can affect the business from a customer service standpoint. Correct logging of inventory can also have an impact on revenue and customer service—for example, if your company were to unexpectedly run out of an item. For service businesses, this could be materials and supplies that are needed to perform the work. For retail businesses, this would be the actual products sold. Not only does an inventory system prevent outages; it can also increase the efficiency of dollars used in inventory supply.

Human resources processes are some of the most important to establish as the business grows and starts adding employees. Since the greatest influence on your business is the people who do the work and run it, the emphasis on these processes cannot be understated. If you, as a business leader, have plans to grow the business, work on this system and its processes well before you believe it is necessary. Establish and document roles and responsibilities (job descriptions), create an employee handbook with all the policies you anticipate you will need, design an employee agreement, build an onboarding process, and implement a process to measure and monitor performance to reward or discipline employees as required.

The *financial* system and its supporting processes are intertwined with many other functions of the business. They should be tied into sales (revenue), payroll, inventory (cost of goods), customer service (returns or corrections), and operations (costs), along with many other functions depending on the business type. The finance system must be robust—and the processes, clearly defined—so the flow of information is seamless and as automated as possible.

Payroll is a system that can be highly automated if the proper resource is chosen for the business. This can either be outsourced or conducted in house. Some easily managed payroll systems within accounting packages that small businesses can use include Quick-Books and ADP.

The *legal system* for a business may be very simple or complex depending on the needs of the business. Many companies outsource all their legal needs to a firm on retainer or via a legal service. One legal service we recommend is LegalShield. We have found it to be an inexpensive option for small businesses. If you'd like more information, see the appendix.

Customer service may be part of the job of each person within the business. I tend to think it should be the responsibility of each employee to provide thorough customer service, rather than having a sole department to address customer issues. However, some businesses require a customer service team or system. This is typically linked to sales, and sometimes operations, to facilitate communication and problem resolution.

IT has quickly become a necessity in today's business climate. Computers, internet, and other technology have become a part of what is expected by customers, vendors, and business partners. For small to medium businesses, these are easily outsourced to other companies. However, IT is important, as this functional area supports all other systems.

Operations is typically the backbone of any business. Whether it's a service business, a manufacturer, or even an online business, there is an aspect of operations that needs to be considered. This is generally how the product or service is created and delivered to the end user. This is a critical system and function.

THE VALUE OF PROCESSES

It is important to realize what constitutes a solid documented process or system. There are some criteria that make up a solid documented process. If processes are missing, one or more of these criteria will be in jeopardy. Let's walk through each of the following criteria for a process:

1. It supports the people who are following it.

2. It is continually improved.

3. It is as efficient as possible.

4. It is easily understood.

5. The results are visible to stakeholders.

6. It supports the values of the organization.

7. It delivers value to the customer.

A process should support the people using it in several ways. It must make the job at hand easier to accomplish. A well-thought-out process will make the activities flow in the proper order and with clarity. It will also provide a step-by-step method for training purposes.

The continual improvement of a process or system is important to the efficiency and effectiveness of the organization. The ideas of the system managers and the people who are using the processes should be reviewed periodically and adopted when appropriate. The continuous-improvement actions, when implemented, will increase efficiency, which in turn should add value to the customer, either through speed or accuracy—or both.

Extra steps and wasted actions should be removed as the process is reviewed. The use of automation, where it is applicable, can also be beneficial. Creating a current-state map of the process and then creating a future state with marked efficiency improvements is a common way to simplify a process.

For a process or system to be adopted and followed, it must be simple to understand. If it cannot be written down and explained by all stakeholders, then it isn't easily understood. This is critical to sustaining the momentum of using a process, especially when it is new to a small business.

The results of a system or process must be visible to all stakeholders regardless of what form they take, be it KPIs, goals or metrics, a dashboard, or something else. As the axiom goes, "If you can't measure it, you can't manage it." So goes the power of the process.

The values of the organization must ring true in all aspects of the business but especially within the processes built to drive the business activities. If a process runs counter to the outcome directed by the company values, inconsistency exists, and the results will benefit neither the customer nor the brand.

The processes and systems must add value to the customer, no matter if that individual is internal or external. If a system or process does not add value to a customer, it is a waste and should be reviewed and adjusted immediately.

In effect, if your business does not formulate and document processes, you are at the mercy of tribal knowledge. Tribal knowledge can be defined as the inherent way things are known to be accomplished by the people who exist within an organization. A business can run on tribal knowledge while it is very small or for a determined period of time, but eventually, this type of thinking will lead to mistakes, confusion, and chaos. Tribal knowledge is used to build processes; it is not a process or system within itself. If your business does not create and implement proper systems, you will be at the mercy of tribal knowledge. Tribal knowledge leaves a business as experienced employees depart, so as an owner, you must solidify your business by building out the processes.

Tribal knowledge is how some very small businesses operate, and many do so successfully for years or even the life span of the business. These businesses generally have no plans to grow beyond a few employees. However, I don't suggest reliance on tribal knowledge as a long-term strategy. Your business can run more efficiently and effectively with solid systems and processes in place. They will allow you to grow and scale without being limited. To be successful, you really need a leaner, faster, smarter business.

FROM TRIBAL KNOWLEDGE TO AN OPERATING SYSTEM

I recently worked with a small business named SCA, made up of approximately fifty employees. SCA had reached the point in their growth curve at which they had outgrown their tribal knowledge. This meant they were too large to efficiently share necessary knowledge using word of mouth. They were sacrificing speed, accuracy, and costs by using this limited, often misinterpreted, form of company communication. They were also limiting their growth potential. What they needed were defined processes, SOPs, and systems. Of course, from their perspective, creating these processes amounted to a monumental task.

When this business was made up of eight or nine people, the idea of creating written job descriptions, documenting roles and responsibilities, and putting together the SOPs seemed like overkill and a waste of time. They couldn't imagine that they would reference the material or how it would help them in doing their jobs. In that short-term thinking, it was easy to justify putting off the inevitable. The thought, *It just doesn't have to be done today*, was apparent in their attitudes and actions.

Eventually, they reached out to me to help change their business and implement a growth strategy. Where we began, after creating their vision story and laying out the goals and objectives of the business, was in the area of processes and systems. We did a thorough review of the current state of their processes, and we found that tribal knowledge reigned supreme. This opened them up to a huge potential for error and an inability to hold anyone accountable.

We started documenting their processes by interviewing those who had the tribal knowledge. In doing so, we found that different opinions existed about these processes, which added another layer of complexity. So, in documenting the processes, we had to reach a consensus on what the current processes should be. Is it any wonder the company had so much inefficient activity? When surrounded by tribal knowledge with differing opinions, it stands to reason that consistency is lacking.

The team from SCA decided that the human resources and training processes were the most important places to start. The lack of a recruiting process, an onboarding process, a documented employee manual, and an expense-reporting SOP were the most critical priorities. They chose these because of the emphasis they placed on the people they needed to hire to sustain their growth.

We then took each process and mapped a future state. In doing so, we made sure the process was as efficient as could be within the current systems and with the tools available. As the future states were agreed upon, we documented the process. SOPs were created as needed.

An intentional effort to train the employees on these new processes ensued. Creating a new process and documenting it are just the first steps. The process also must be communicated to employees, and training must occur. It is important to explain to all stakeholders about following the process and why it is so critical to do so.

As these processes were put into place at SCA, some expected— but interesting—events occurred. First, the functions that had new processes developed began running much more smoothly and efficiently than ever before. Second, the visibility of the processes and the outcomes helped to communicate to management that those areas of the business were under control. Last but not least, especially from my coaching viewpoint, the team was clamoring to define and document more processes within the business because they'd seen the great benefit of doing so.

The team at SCA has now embarked on a journey of continuous improvement in regard to processes and systems. They are constantly looking for better tools, process improvements, and rejuvenated systems. It has become a part of their culture. This way of thinking will assist them in their continued quest for growth.

CHANGE FOR THE BETTER

As far as business processes and systems are concerned, they are to be built and maintained with continuous-improvement methods. Things change, and these changes need to be constantly reviewed. Reviewing ensures that the systems and processes that were once put into effect are still the best paths for the business to follow. Through rapid technology improvements and changing client expectations, systems and processes can become obsolete. Using continuous-improvement methods to identify wastes in the processes is critical.

However, it is critical that each process in question be clearly defined and mapped before the continuous-improvement activity. The *current state* of the process must be documented before figuring out what it should become. The current process, no matter how crude or defined it may be, is the standard that has been set in the organization. The goal is to review that process and determine if improvements can be made.

The improvement process is sometimes called a *kaizen activity*. *Kaizen* is a Sino-Japanese word that means change for the better or improvement.

"Where there is no standard, there can be no kaizen."

—Taiichi Ohno, Japanese industrial engineer and creator of the Toyota Production System

HOW TO IMPROVE A PROCESS

1. Document the current process, called the *current-state map* or *value stream*. Do this by interviewing all stakeholders in this process. It may be just one person or two, or a great number of people, depending on the process. It is also valuable to interview a customer involved in the process.

2. Create a future-state map to visualize what the process will look like once the identified changes are made. This map is based on the findings through review of the current state and identification of needed improvements.

3. Identify the gaps between the current-state map and the future-state map, and take action. The actions to be taken to move from the current state to the future state need to be specific, measurable, achievable, realistic, and time bound (SMART goals).

The owner of a business must make a conscious decision on whether to grow or remain at the current business level. This is where many business owners find a business coach very useful. Sometimes a guide is needed to help you see what you cannot see on your own. You don't know what you don't know.

Chapter 6

PEOPLE POWER

What is the greatest asset of your business—and usually, the greatest cost to a business? Your people. They are what make the business what it is. They are a reflection of the business. People either make or break a business; they either support systems and processes, or they choose to be less than engaged.

It all starts with your leadership and expectations and how they translate to the workforce.

At the end of your time on earth, there is one clear and simple way that people will describe you: how you treated others. That is what others will remember first and last about you, good or bad. They will remember how you made them feel.

TREATING A PERSON AS IF HE OR SHE IS SPECIAL

My father, Dewey Gray, owned and operated Gray & Associates Engineers, LLC. He was a brilliant electrical engineer with his professional engineering license, a master's degree, and many awards and achievements. He ran the business for more than thirty years and had numerous clients, many who became repeat clients. He never had to advertise or market the business after the initial start-up because the work he and his team produced was fantastic. The business literally sold itself.

When my father passed away in spring 2015, the truth about his life was revealed. As his son, I, of course, knew how loving and compassionate he was. It was easy for me to set aside all his professional accolades and see him as a caring person.

What truly blew me away, and still does to this day, was the resounding message we received from others about him after his death. Person after person told my family and me about the care and love he had shown them. They would talk about things he had said or done specifically for them. It was as if each person thought he or she was the only one who'd had that deep relationship with him. He made everyone feel genuinely special.

Now that is extraordinary in itself; however, the people I am referring to are members of his business team and his customers. These are colleagues who were peers and employees. They all thought he did a great job for them, of course, but at the end of his time on this earth, what they remembered and felt about him was his *love and care* for them. The stories came pouring in from everywhere about how he had affected others. He truly left a legacy.

Yes, business is about income, profits, and all the accomplishments we describe as business success, but it can and should also be about our relationship with others. How we treat people, and—more importantly—how we love and care for people is a true gauge of who we are or have been. The way we treat employees, customers, vendors, or anyone we encounter during our business ventures will influence others positively or negatively. We have the opportunity to construct a legacy full of positive interactions with others.

*"We make a living by what we get, but we
make a life by what we give."*

—**Unknown**

THE POWER OF PEOPLE IN CHANGING CULTURE

Eventually all small-business owners realize the most important asset of their business is its people. This is the case for a client I worked with in the manufacturing space, FDW. While this company had been in business for over twenty years, the owners decided it was time for them to step back from the day-to-day operations and build a dynamic high-performance team to run the business. They felt that it was time to hire a GM, based on the V&I premise. They agreed that it was critical to find and recruit the right people into the business so they could prepare for a transition and new growth stage.

We started by addressing the current hiring process. We created a current-state map of their process, which was tribal knowledge, by the way. Then we outlined a new hiring process from start to finish.

We identified what FDW was doing to ensure they hired people who could not only do the job but who also had the skills and culture fit the company desired. We quickly determined that they were not doing what they should to qualify new hires. They were conducting interviews and even doing some background checks; however, they were experiencing a higher turnover than they desired and dissatisfaction with the overall results. To improve their system, we implemented personality profiles, a more robust interview process, and a skills review. What resulted from this was a more intentional hiring process and a more qualified and engaged team.

Along with the new hiring practice, we implemented a thorough onboarding process and clearly outlined culture expectations. Once the correct new hires were found, we wanted to emphasize the proper behaviors to be sure that they would get off on the right foot. FDW strives to create a culture that supports high customer support and satisfaction.

We implemented incentives and metrics to drive the proper behaviors. Incentives for all employees revolved around customer satisfaction and job performance. Training on expected attitudes and culture was also put in place.

Another area we worked on was leadership development with the new GM. FDW ultimately decided to move someone from inside the organization into this important role. To develop a high-performance team, leadership skills are critical. Being able to communicate expectations clearly and hold people accountable is a must. Part of what we determined was that while most of the employees could be upgraded through the new hiring practices, there were some employees with the proper fit who had left due to lack of leadership.

As the proper hiring practices were put into place, things began to change for the positive. The culture started to improve, beginning with leadership of the company. We also noticed that newly hired employees spoke highly of the environment and recommended to others that they join the company. This is one of the best ways to find new employees who are the right fit and was a sure sign that the company culture was improving.

FDW did not even have to increase the pay rate to achieve the overall results they desired.

THE IMPORTANCE OF PEOPLE

The people in your company *are* your company. They are the attitude, the brand, and the energy. They are those who get the work done. They are those who affect the customer directly. They are the present and the future of the business. The importance of the people in your business should never be underestimated.

The attitude of your employees directly affects your customers, especially for those employees performing services for or speaking directly with customers in customer-support roles. Your customers can sense a lack of empowerment in your employees. If you don't trust your employees to make decisions for your customers, you've either hired the wrong people or you have some work to do from a leadership perspective.

Your employees also represent your brand. The brand is the actions, attitudes, and culture that show through to the customers. You can market a brand all day long, but the brand is what the customer experiences. This experience is the result of the interaction between the employees and the customers.

Your employees are key to the future of your business. The improvement activities surrounding your processes and systems, as well as product and service enhancements, will largely come from the workforce. Business growth will be affected greatly, either positively or negatively, by the teammates who are working in and on the business.

"Achievement comes to someone when he is able to do great things for himself. Success comes when he empowers followers to do great things with him. Significance comes when he develops leaders to do great things for him. But legacy is created only when a person puts his organization into the position to do great things without him."

—John C. Maxwell, American author, speaker, and pastor

GROW THE PEOPLE, GROW THE BUSINESS

The growth of the individuals in the business directly correlates to the growth of the business. A company that invests in the development of its employees will not only create better employees; it will also create a better business. Many times, a common question arises with business owners when we discuss this: "What if we train them and then they leave?" Of course, their concern is the expense spent on employee development. My response is always that it is the right investment to make, regardless.

Why do I say this? First, if you invest in employees, they are less likely to leave. Unless you have other issues, such as a toxic culture, showing them that they are important by investing in them is positive for engagement. Second, if you don't train them and they don't improve on their own, then your company will stagnate. The small amount of money saved by not investing in your employees is not worth the risk of eroding continuous improvement of your business. It is important to the company culture to make this an integral part of the business plan.

HOW TO CREATE EMPLOYEE ENGAGEMENT FOR HIGH PERFORMANCE

1. Create proper incentives. Bonuses, rewards, and incentives must be structured correctly. They need to correlate to behaviors, performance, and results. They must be clearly understood, visible, and easily measured.

2. Care for your employees. There is nothing more important or rewarding than truly caring for your people. This means having

compassion for them as human beings. This cannot be faked or manipulated in any way and must come from the leader's heart.

3. Facilitate fun. One of your business values should be to have fun. Working hard and having fun are not in opposition to each other. As a matter of fact, some recent studies show that having fun is both productive and increases engagement.

4. Allow employees to express themselves. Everyone has a deep desire to belong. All people want to be themselves. By promoting this freedom to your employees, you are creating a culture of acceptance and empowerment.

5. Lead by example. What a leader does speaks louder than what a leader says. It is just that simple.

6. Communicate, communicate, communicate. Proper communication is essential for any group of people. When things go awry, it can usually be traced back to a lack of appropriate communication.

7. Ask for feedback and listen. Affording others the opportunity to give feedback is immeasurably important. It shows you care, it proves they are valuable, and it improves an organization. Listening is a key part of the communication process.

8. Empower employees to wow the customer. The best way to wow the customer is by allowing employees to make on-the-spot decisions. Of course, you can give parameters; however, when they make decisions, support them. If they mess up, teach them.

9. Provide development opportunities. Most people want to continue to improve themselves. Giving employees an oppor-

tunity to grow and learn is a great way to show you care about them, and it, in turn, improves the company as a whole.

10. Build trust. Without trust, nothing else matters. The bedrock of all high-performing teams is trust. It cannot be bought or negotiated. It can only be *given,* and it must be earned.

11. Provide challenging work. People who have the ability to perform at a high level crave the opportunity to be challenged. Delegate to them responsibility, hold them accountable, and support them. They will flourish.

12. Establish clear KPIs. Providing clarity in how they are measured, why they are specifically important, and how they are managed is critical.

13. Recognize high performance. A business must define what high performance looks like within each role and responsibility document. It must be made clear to the employees, who should then be recognized for it as well.

14. Create a high-performance culture. The culture of the organization is the factor that differentiates it from other businesses, whether or not they are direct competitors. It is the heartbeat of the business and can be felt by all.

EXTERNAL PEOPLE

There are other people who greatly influence the success of a company: the external resources, such as vendors and suppliers. Attorneys, certified public accountants (CPAs), financial planners, consultants, and business advisers, among others, are individuals with whom it is important to engage to have a successful, growing business. It is crucial to establish external resources, especially as a small business, as many of these roles can't be supportedby payroll. It is much more efficient and effective to outsource specialized and professional tasks.

ATTORNEY: There are a few ways to line up an attorney to support your business—for instance, working with a local attorney on retainer, through a national organization, through a monthly stipend, or through a legal service for a low monthly fee. If you are working in a franchise organization, there are attorneys who specialize in this area. An attorney's expertise is essential to support your business goals. An attorney should be able to review business contracts, discuss employment laws, and guide you in your business entity and tax laws.

CPA: In a small business, a CPA is used much like a controller in addition to being an accountant. They can guide you strategically to prevent large costs and to prepare for the future growth of your business. They can advise you on tax strategy and entity choice, among other things. Most importantly, they free you to do the work you need to do to grow your business.

CONSULTANT: Small-business consultants can be a very valuable asset to your business, especially as you enter a growth phase. They see things that you may not have the foresight or experience to see. They will help you set up processes and systems based on their experience and knowledge. They can save you time and expedite preparation for growth. They should not, however, be so entrenched in the business that you don't completely understand what they are doing. Make sure you are clear with them about this on the front end. As a consultant, I solve a specific problem and then move on.

COACH: Business and personal coaches can be a real blessing to a small-business owner. The difference between a coach and a consultant is one of focus. While a consultant is working on a specific problem, set of data, or process, a coach is an adviser of sorts. A small-business coach should coach you not only on your business but also on yourself. This is a more holistic approach to success. As a coach, I work on the life plan of the business owner and the vision story for the business. Then I help him or her structure a successful business and personal life to make that happen.

HUMAN RESOURCES EXPERT OR TEAM: For you, as a business owner with the growth of your business as a goal, outsourcing many of the human resource functions can be a freeing experience. There are many laws and regulations that can easily be misunderstood by or unknown to a business owner. A human resources firm can make the process timelier and more efficient. One word of caution: Never outsource the hiring process. You can get help in recruiting and even managing the process; however, you, as the business owner, are ultimately responsible for bringing in the right people. You must take the lead in the hiring process because your employees are your business.

MARKETING EXPERT OR TEAM: With social media being a driving focus in the marketing world today, it makes sense that some, if not all, of your marketing functions should be outsourced. While there is some use of traditional media in the marketing plans, even that is likely better outsourced, from a time and cost perspective.

There are some very good small firms that can handle your marketing strategy once you agree on a plan. The caveat is that you must work with the firm to create that plan and remain accountable for it. Have the firm agree to a weekly status meeting. They must provide objective evidence of what is being done and the progress that has been made toward the goal. You must know what is and isn't working.

TECHNOLOGY EXPERT OR TEAM: It is imperative in today's world that the technology supporting your business is always functioning. Not only that, but it also needs to be updated and maintained on a regular basis. Finding a technology support team external to your small business is important. It would be great to have a team local to you—although it's not necessary these days—so they can help you through emergencies and get you back up and running should something fail. The key here is to make sure you have a plan for regular upgrades so you stay abreast of technology needed to efficiently run your business with as little interruption as possible. Cloud-based systems are very common today. They offer a lot of flexibility and ease of use for you and your customer. They also have redundancy built in. You also need contingency plans when things do go wrong. Redundant systems, replacement equipment, and alternate options should all be considered part of a technology plan. Last but not least, don't forget cyber-security concerns, especially if you have a major online presence. This company will likely be different from your hardware and IT resources.

FINDING YOUR OUTSOURCE PARTNER

Recently, while working with Aaron Wyssmann, owner of Ozarks Remodeling, a highly recommended construction company in Springfield, Missouri, we found a few opportunities for which they could use some external vendors. They decided to outsource three specific processes: marketing, bookkeeping, and inbound sales calls. The purpose of outsourcing was to delegate low-energy items the business owner was doing and to allow for expansion as the business grows.

They asked for recommendations from other businesses, conducted interviews, and performed reference checks. Eventually they found their new vendors. They provided the documented processes and KPIs to be measured, just like they would with an employee. In reality, a vendor is an extension of your business and your processes.

They tried three different bookkeepers on a limited basis until they found the one who fit their expectations and made them a member of their team. Always be prepared to run a trial period with a vendor before you sign a contract or agree to a long-term arrangement.

They found a virtual assistant to conduct the inbound sales calls process. The business owner found that by prescribing a step-by-step process with a decision tree for specific questions, the calls were answered exceptionally well and at a greater frequency than what had previously been possible.

The marketing processes had been a thorn in their side for the past year or so. Each marketing company made results promises that they did not keep. Ozarks Remodeling had switched marketing companies several times. We found that they needed a vendor able to focus on a couple of specific strategies. They decided to choose a small firm that could give them the weekly accountability and results they desired.

By outsourcing these three processes to the right vendors, they made progress. The best part about it was the business owner and the team were able to focus on what they do best without the worry of these processes hanging over their heads.

They are now looking to delegate or outsource the estimation process. They have yet to determine whether they will hire an employee or outsource to a vendor. Either way, it is another step in the right direction as they continue to prepare for growth by moving responsibility to the most capable and efficient people.

WHAT THE BUSINESS OWNER THINKS

"Like many business owners I talk to, I believed that with my business, there was no way I would be able to systematize it. The reason I thought this was that I wrongfully believed that I was the one needing to make most if not all of the decisions; after all, no one knows my business like I do. The problem with this thinking is that I was chained to my business. What I have since learned is that what I must do is teach others how I think about the decisions and then trust that they will do at least 80 percent as well as I do.

"The first place I started was using technology out in the field, so that information could instantly be sent out by my virtual assistant to my subcontractors. Next, I handed off to my virtual assistant answering all our company's inbound telephone calls. Again, I used technology to teach her the exact questions I ask and the type of information I was looking for. I now believe that she does a much better job than I ever did, and she has such a sweet tone. No one knows that she is three states away from where I operate my business. I still struggle from time to time in believing that the more complicated parts of my business can be systematized, but just last week I did it on probably the most complicated part. It felt great handing it off, as I have bought myself at least twenty hours per week that I can use to do the other parts of my business that I love or spend more time with my family. My immediate goal is to become completely replaceable and to have my business run with those I've trained and trust to make as good, if not better, decisions than I would make."

—**Aaron Wyssmann**

RECOMMENDED RECRUITING AND HIRING PROCESS

As the people you bring into your company are important to your future success, the hiring process should produce the right results. Spend time documenting the process, working the process, and improving the process until your team sees the quality results desired. Below I outline a couple of successful processes we have implemented in some variation with different clients. You need to make sure that the hiring process makes sense for your business. Use the following as a guide, but be sure to design it to fit your needs. Keep working on it until you get the consistent results your business requires.

Key Employee Processes (managers, customer-facing positions, and executives)

- Recruit with specific roles and responsibilities outlined.

- Ask for written responses.

- Conduct phone interviews—multiple if necessary.

- Schedule face-to-face interviews—as many as needed.

- Complete personality profiles and/or skills assessments.

- Gather background and reference checks.

- Look them up on social media.

- Invite them to lunch or dinner (spouse included).

- Use technology in the process.

- Set clear culture expectations.

All Employees Process (hourly workers, laborers, non-customer-facing positions)

- Recruit with job description.

- Conduct phone interviews.

- Conduct face-to-face interviews.

- Conduct background and reference checks.

- Look them up on social media.

- Conduct skills assessments.

- Set clear culture expectations.

The steps in the hiring process are mostly self-explanatory; however, let's discuss a few of them. Phone interviews are critical, as they can save your team time by screening those who do not fit the profile of the employee you are looking for. Another reason for the phone interview is to assess a candidate's skill in that area. Sometimes people who can pass a face-to-face interview have poor phone etiquette.

The face-to-face interview is the most common and sometimes only method used to judge potential employees. While it is important, it is not the only step your business should be taking. Do not fall into the trap of becoming enamored with an interviewee through a face-to-face interview and forsake all the other pieces of information you should be using.

Background checks, reference checks, and social media searches are some of the most effective ways to find out the truth about a candidate. We have seen them eliminate many candidates who would have otherwise made the cut. Do not skip these steps, as you may regret doing so.

The lunch or dinner interview, with the spouse included, is the secret step. By the time you get to this step, you are likely very interested in hiring this individual. For key positions, it is critical that you get to know the real person who will join your team. The spouse or significant other plays a big role in a person's character and behaviors. If the individual acts dramatically different around their spouse, be wary. Either move on or, at the very least, investigate further.

WHY ASSESSMENTS?

There are a few reasons you should consider using assessments. They are helpful in providing an honest profile of the person you are considering for employment or contract work.

The interview process, while important, gives you only so much insight into the personality and behavior tendencies of an individual. A personality profile, skills profile, and other types of assessments can help eliminate guesswork and assumptions about people. Remember these individuals will represent your company and your brand and directly affect your customers.

We use the DiSC profile with each of our clients. For more information, refer to the appendix. The main reason we prefer the DiSC is that it is simple to understand and is based on predicted behaviors that the person will exhibit. Understanding an individual's behaviors and preferred communication style is indispensable in determining role fit and, ultimately, performance.

Your people are an asset but even more of an investment. They may show up as an expense or cost on the P&L and don't show up as an asset on the balance sheet, but they are still the company's greatest investment!

ORGANIZATIONAL CHARTS

An organizational chart (org chart), or what we like to call a *people plan*, is an important piece of the process of designing the people part of the business. As in all aspects of the business, it is important to create a visual representation for the SOP. An org chart is a way to visually communicate the reporting relationships and the individuals in the roles of each system and process of the organization. In small companies and start-ups, it is common for one person to have multiple roles. For example, the CEO, owner, and CFO may be the same person. That person may also conduct sales for a period of time. The goal is to eventually grow the business so that each role is filled by a different and better-qualified individual.

An org chart can also be used as a plan for future growth and strategic hiring. There may be many roles that are in the vision for the future. Even if you have only one or two people in the business right now, do not skip the step of developing an org chart.

To develop an org chart, start with the systems of the business—the functional departments. For example, you may have sales, finance, human resources, and operations as the business's functional areas. List these across the page horizontally underneath the owner (visionary) or GM (integrator) role, if you have implemented the V&I concept. Do not use people's names just yet. We will work through this process by being people agnostic. You can identify the people who fill these roles later.

Add the business processes under each functional area, or system, of the business. List each process of your business vertically underneath the system in which it belongs. Each process must fit below one of the systems; if this is not the case, you may be missing a system.

The system manager will be responsible for ensuring the processes are performing as they should. Eventually, each process must have a role responsible for and accountable to it. This could be the manager or a member of his or her team. The key is to make sure you have accounted for each system and each process that your business requires.

Once you have developed the org chart, you can see how your business should be organized based on your current needs. You can go through this exercise by creating a current-state org chart (how it looks today) and a future-state org chart (the plan for growth). As your business grows, you will likely add processes and possibly even systems.

To account for outsourced processes and systems, you can add them to the org chart in dotted lines. This way, you can see that they are outsourced, even though someone in your organization is responsible for their performance. In your future-state org chart, you may want to bring some of these roles in house. Just don't lose sight of all your processes, even if they're outsourced.

ORG CHART TEMPLATE

Create your org chart from a system and process standpoint. Do not place people's names on the chart just yet. It is important to identify each system, or functional area, of the business first and then identify each and every process that falls within each system. Eventually you will need to be sure that each process has a process leader and responsible party. That will be identified and included on each role and responsibility document. Again, one person may be covering several processes and even systems, especially at the creation of your business and through its first few years of growth.

CARE AT ALL COST

"A company is stronger if it is bound by love rather than by fear. If the employees come first, then they are happy."

—Herb Kelleher, cofounder of Southwest Airlines

The idea of caring for your employees and people who touch your organization—vendors, customers, and others—is not a new concept nor a difficult one to understand. However, it is not as common a practice as it should be. Many business leaders and owners remain stuck in the command-and-control style of management. That does work and has for a long time; however, it is short sighted and a lazy way to lead. Fear and control will get the troops moving, but they will never be engaged to the extent the business needs them to be. The people will not find true joy in their work when they do not feel the love and care that they need. People today, in all aspects of their lives, are yearning for leaders who care for them and look out for them. Let's be clear, however: we are not talking about letting the troops take control or be allowed to make inappropriate demands of a business. What we are talking about is loving the people for who they are. The interesting truth of this is that *not* caring can cost your business a lot, but it costs nothing to care.

ROLES AND RESPONSIBILITIES

Every small business needs to develop clear roles and responsibilities (job descriptions) for every system within the business. Each system is made up of several processes, and each process subsequently needs to be accounted for by each of the roles developed.

When developing roles and responsibilities, do not use the current people within your organization as a guide. Clear your mind of your current team members, and create the roles as they are intended to be to meet the needs of your vision, mission, and values.

EXAMPLE ROLE AND RESPONSIBILITY

ROLE TITLE	SALES MANAGER
REPORTS TO	OWNER

ROLE PURPOSE

The sales manager is responsible for providing sales and customer service support to all clients.

MISSION AND VALUES

Mission Statement
Core Values

DUTIES AND RESPONSIBILITIES

The primary responsibilities of the sales manager include the following:

- Support mission and values 100 percent of the time

- Manage sales strategy to increase net income with growth in margin and revenue

- Train, educate, and mentor new and existing sales and sales-support personnel

- Track and report sales metrics and KPIs

- Make and receive sales calls, and document interactions in the CRM

- Recruit and dismiss staff as warranted

- Prepare and process sales agreements

- Prepare and plan special events

- Ensure and measure customer satisfaction scores

- Attend meetings as scheduled

- Adhere to all company policies, procedures, and business-ethics codes, and ensure that they are communicated and implemented within the team

- Perform other duties as assigned

QUALIFICATIONS

- The ideal candidate will have the following qualifications:

- A minimum of three years' experience in a leadership role

- Proficient in Microsoft Office

- Familiar with using a CRM (a plus)

- Organized and self-motivated

- Driven and self-directed sales professional

- Exceptional communication skills, presentation skills, negotiation and management skills, strong work ethic, positive attitude, and professional demeanor (required)

- Advanced networking ability and existing relationships in the industry (preferred)

- Proven people skills with effective experience in training, managing, and mentoring

- Ability to set and meet sales goals

WORKING CONDITIONS

This is an office position. The sales manager will have access to the internet and be able to coordinate with other team members across the country in different time zones as needed.

PHYSICAL REQUIREMENTS

The role requires standing for extended periods of time, lifting heavy objects greater than forty pounds, and driving regularly.

THE ULTIMATE LEVERAGE

The ability of a business owner to delegate properly can absolutely change the business. It not only frees the business owner from mundane activities; it also sets the business up for growth. It is a necessity to delegate on an ongoing basis as you grow and scale.

Go back to the delegation process we outlined in chapter 3. Conduct it again for yourself and also for any managers on your team. As you delegate down through the organization, you may need to make room in the list of responsibilities for those taking over your previous responsibilities.

The goal is to always move the activities to the lowest possible level of the organization. This is supported by all the work you have done on processes and systems. With the documented and clearly understood processes, along with effective training, the responsibilities are transferrable.

Chapter 7

A GOAL WITHOUT A PLAN
IS JUST A WISH

"Plans are nothing; planning is everything."

—President Dwight D. Eisenhower

THE FIRST STRATEGIC PLAN

A wonderful client of ours, Dr. Soos Pediatrics in Dublin, Georgia, experienced their first strategic-planning process recently. Dr. Gyula Soos and his wife, Robyn, are the owners. Gyula is the visionary, and Robyn is the integrator. They are prepared to take the business to the next level as the current community leader in their space.

While the business has been in existence for more than ten years, Gyula and Robyn had never conducted a strategic-planning session, at least not the full-blown process that we facilitate and describe here. The business is successful and a great benefit to the community. However, they have opportunities that haven't been realized. Going through a strategic-planning process eliminates those missed opportunities and fuels the team with energy.

This is common for a lot of small businesses, as the need doesn't seem warranted at start-up. Owners become preoccupied with running the business and don't seem to find the time to work on its development. Don't allow your business to fall into this trap, as it allows for missed opportunities. You want to conduct annual strategic-planning reviews to stay ahead of the competition as well.

During the strategic-planning process, expect some frustrations and friction, especially if your business and leadership team have not participated in one before. There are a lot of decisions to be made, and some things that seemed like a priority before the session are eliminated. It's challenging but necessary to wade through the process with the leadership team. You cannot take shortcuts and get the results you desire.

> *"I was very frustrated during the strategy session because there was so much repetition, and I didn't know why ... until I saw the results of what we are doing! And now I am so proud!"*

—Robyn Soos, co-owner, Dr. Soos Pediatrics

Dr. Soos Pediatrics is a profitable business and does many great things; however, they found themselves in a prioritization quandary. The owners and team members have a lot of tremendously good ideas on a regular basis—so many, in fact, that they had become paralyzed about which ones to act upon. The leadership team also wasn't clear on the priorities or the mission of the clinic. Again, being busy in the business can deflect attention from the strategic planning and implementation.

The place we start in the strategic-planning process is with the vision, mission, and values. Dr. Soos Pediatrics had previously developed a vision story for their business, so we reviewed that with their leadership team at the start of the session. We then went through the process of developing their mission. This alone was eye opening for the team. We then created the company's core values. These are key, as they are the measuring stick for all activities, decisions, and behaviors within the organization. We describe these in more detail below.

The next item we created was a SWOT (strengths, weaknesses, opportunities, and threats) analysis of the business. This helped them to start brainstorming all factors, internal and external, that do or could affect the business. They created an exhaustive list from each of the leadership team members' perspectives. This list is where we eventually identify the three big rocks of a company's strategic plan for the current year and next three years.

Big rocks are the priorities that move the dial toward the vision story for the business. Some big rocks are for the next year, and others are for a longer time frame. The key is to break these down into quarterly priorities so they can be managed by the team. We suggest using a ninety-day periodization framework. The leadership team identified their big rocks and assigned actions to them, beginning with the next quarter, or ninety days.

When setting actions, the team used the simple action listing provided below. In my career, I have seen large companies and divisions run by such a simple tool. There is no need to get elaborate. Just keep it simple and effective. We have added explanations or examples in the visual below:

ACTION #	DESCRIPTION	DUE DATE	RESPONSIBLE PARTY	STATUS
1	OVERALL PROJECT	WHEN DUE	WHO	ON TIME
1A	SUBSET OF PROJECT			COMPLETE
2	ACTION DESCRIPTION			LATE

Another exciting piece of the strategy session we took this leadership team through was the BHAG process. If you haven't heard of it, the BHAG is the "big, hairy, audacious goal." It's like a scary monster, if you will. This is a goal that makes you shudder when you contemplate going after it. It should seem impossible. The Dr. Soos Pediatrics team decided to look ten years into the future and described what would be nearly impossible for them to accomplish. They documented their BHAG and communicated it to their teams.

At this point in the session, we revisited the vision story to see if it remained relevant and accurate, or if changes were needed. The owners did tweak a few things based on the SWOT, the BHAG revelation, and their newly minted mission. It is always wise to revisit the vision story periodically, as things do change as clarity increases.

From all that we had discussed and documented with the team, we decided it was time to develop the brand promise. This is something I rarely see small or even large companies develop. The brand promise is what differentiates you from your competitors, and it is measurable. Being measurable is the key. If you take the BHAG and the mission and distill them into a measurable differentiator, you'll have the brand promise. This team did just that and found a brand promise that fueled their initiatives and actions. It is their calling card internally and externally.

"Always There. Always Care."

—brand promise of Dr. Soos Pediatrics

We then reviewed the KPIs to make sure they aligned with all the discoveries we had made through the strategy session thus far. The KPIs must measure the specific actions and performance of the business so that effective and efficient work is being done in the right areas. It is important to measure the performance of the systems and processes that meet the brand promise and the mission and fulfill the vision story.

WHY SPEND TIME AND ENERGY ON STRATEGY?

There is a common adage that plans are outdated the moment they are completed. In many cases, this is true. However, the act of planning and creating a strategy is the most important aspect of putting together a plan. It allows you and your team to walk through different scenarios and your ideal responses. More importantly, it helps you to discuss what you plan *not* to do. It is important to surround yourself with wise counsel and gather input from others, whether they work for your company or not. I often turn to Proverbs 15:22 for guidance here: "Without counsel, plans go wrong, but in the multitude of counselors, they are established." You can create a board of advisers who meet on a predetermined basis to help guide the decisions you and your team ultimately make in the daily running of the business. You can join a mastermind team and speak openly to that team about the challenges and decisions facing your business.

I am currently part of a mastermind team for exactly that reason. The men and women who are part of my team challenge me to think differently, as they propose ideas from perspectives different than my own. It is enlightening and worth every bit of the investment of time and money to be part of such a productive group. Of course, as mentioned earlier, another way to get input and direction is by having a business coach who can challenge your ideas and scenarios as you go through the planning process.

One question I'm frequently asked is, "Why would a small business need a strategic plan?"

It stands to reason with most business owners and leaders that large businesses should spend time developing a strategy. A strategic plan, after all, is complex. These plans are designed to set priorities, focus energy and resources, strengthen operations, ensure the employees and stakeholders are working toward common goals, establish agreement around intended outcomes, and assess the organization's direction in response to a changing environment. It just makes sense that a *Fortune* 500 company would spend time and resources planning its future. It is expected by stockholders, customers, and even the competition.

The question small-business owners are really seeking an answer for is, "Is it worth my time and energy?" That is a good question, but if you think through it, the answer is obvious. *Yes*, it is worth your time and energy, and it is even more important for a small business, as there are limited resources and a smaller margin of error. A small business must make strategic planning an integral part of its business processes. Granted, a small business should not create the amount of output or discovery that a large corporation would; however, the results of the process are critical.

A strategic plan is a road map outlining the necessary steps and actions to get the desired results for the business. Strategy is made up of the conscious choices leaders make to move the organization forward and add value to the customers. It is to guarantee focus is applied to the right actions based on the organizational core values and mission throughout all levels of the organization. As we walk through the components of a strategic plan, the clarity that comes from the process will be apparent. Remember that the plan itself is not as important as the process you go through, the planning. It is the challenging and awakening of the mind that is the key to the planning process.

There are many things that need to be considered in an overall business strategy. There are external factors and internal factors that can influence business success. While it may seem that the small business would be less influenced by these factors, the reality is that they can be affected with equal or greater consequences than a large corporation can.

A small business doesn't usually have a diverse portfolio of revenue-generating businesses or investments to hedge the risks. Some of the factors to consider are the economic environment, advancements in technology, political forces, and social trends. These are overarching and fall into the "broad environment," as described in *Foundations of Strategic Management* by Jeffrey S. Harrison and Caron H. St. John. While the small-business owner and leader cannot control these factors, they still need to be aware of them and consider them in the strategic-planning process.

Some more commonly considered external factors are competitors, suppliers, local government, financial institutions, and customers. These are typically what business leaders think of when they are asked to consider the key pieces for a business strategy. These are important to keep in mind when developing a strategy because they affect the day-to-day workings of the business and are a critical part of its processes.

Internal factors of a business strategy include issues that are within the control of the organization, such as the owners, employees, managers, and advisers. Also included are the company resources, whether a financial asset, a hard asset, or an intrinsic asset—such as a brand.

THE BASIC COMPONENTS OF AN EFFECTIVE STRATEGY ARE AS FOLLOWS:

- Current strategy assessment

- Customers and stakeholders

- Vision and future assumptions

- Mission and purpose

- Values

- Competitive advantage and analysis

- Strengths and weaknesses analysis

- Long-term objectives/strategic direction

- Actions, time line, and results

As a small-business owner or leader, you may find these basic components overwhelming. This is one reason why it is beneficial to involve your team in your strategic planning.

Break it up into parts. Assign groups to address one or two of these components, and then give the groups time to evaluate and brainstorm. Once that is accomplished, reunite as a team and discuss these basic and vital elements of your business.

All members of your team will be empowered through their participation and, as a result, will feel free to voice their own ideas and embrace the team's outcomes. Following are some suggested questions for your team to consider when reworking the current strategy process.

CURRENT STRATEGY ASSESSMENT

1. What is the business's vision over the short term and long term?

2. What external factors are affecting the business?

3. What internal factors are affecting the business?

4. What unique value does your business add to the marketplace?

5. How is the marketplace changing? What are the current trends?

6. What value does your business add that offers a competitive advantage?

7. What is your business's purpose statement?

8. What are the current top three objectives for this fiscal year?

9. Have you conducted SWOT analysis of your current strategy?

The assessment should bring to light for you one of a few results. You will have a well-defined strategy, no strategy at all, or one that needs work. Most likely you have some sort of strategy, even if it is only in your mind. If you were to ask everyone in your organization to answer these questions, would the answers be consistent? The key is to have everyone in the organization be clear about the strategic direction and the resulting actions they need to take on a daily basis. What they do daily is either congruent with or outside the intent of the business strategy. The goal is, of course, to keep all people aligned with the planned action and the desired results. That is what a strategy is designed to do.

Customers are individuals or groups who use the business's products or services. The stakeholders are people who have a vested interest in the success of that business, such as vendors, employees, owners, partners, affiliates, stockholders, and investors. It is important that these are clearly identified and agreed to by the team putting together the strategy. Determine what each stakeholder and customer expects from the business and any key factors in the relationship.

"Strategic planning is worthless—unless there is first a strategic vision."

—John Naisbitt, American author

A vision is what the organization desires to become. It sets a defined direction for the intended growth and accomplishments. The members of an organization must have a clear and compelling vision of what they want their organization to become. Part of setting that vision is looking into the future. This should be part of the strategy discussion. Take some time and investigate the market conditions and trends that are changing the industry or business environment.

Identify the critical technological, environmental, and economic changes that will have an impact on the future. Look deep into the industry in which you live and work, paying special attention to the evolving or emerging marketplace. Set a vision that considers the inherent potential aspects of the company and the intentional desires the organization has around what it will become.

A mission and purpose define an organization. The mission is why the organization exists. A market-driven mission is inherently more successful than an internally driven plan or even a customer-focused plan. The mission is the summary of the guiding values.

The purpose is the reason for being. It aligns with the values and is the defining meaning for this business. It should inspire the people of the organization and those connected to the organization by providing a deeper motivation to do the all-important work.

Keep the following guidelines in mind when developing a mission statement and purpose statement:

1. Be brief.

2. Keep it simple.

3. Focus.

4. Look into the future.

5. Make the statements easily understood.

6. Inspire greatness.

7. Provide clear direction.

Values are guiding principles. They are the bedrock of a culture. The defining values of an organization must support the vision, mission, and purpose. Values and the corresponding culture are, in essence, the spirit of the business and will either enhance or erode the momentum toward achieving the strategic objectives. A business with a vision, mission, and purpose that are aligned with its core values and supported by the appropriate culture will find the people who will bring their best and be inspired. This will result in an engaged workforce and a business that is accomplishing its mission.

Keep the following guidelines in mind when developing your organization's values:

1. The values make up the spirit of the organization.

2. They are not negotiable.

3. They are unchanging truths.

4. They clearly define the expected culture.

5. They support integrity.

6. They set expectations for individual behavior.

7. They provide wisdom for decision-making.

COMPETITIVE ADVANTAGE AND ANALYSIS

Perform a SWOT analysis on the current competitors. A SWOT analysis is a tool used to determine the strengths, weaknesses, opportunities, and threats of an organization. Each of the external and internal factors of a business strategy will be used within the development of a SWOT analysis for your business. Strengths are internal resources that can enhance the competitive advantage of the organization. Weaknesses are internal resources that are inefficient but needed by the organization to remain in a competitive state. Opportunities are external factors that can be used by the business to enhance its competitive advantages. Threats are external factors that are identified as potential impediments to reaching planned results.
SWOT Analysis

STRENGTHS	WEAKNESSES
OPPORTUNITIES	THREATS

The horizontal axis of the chart represents environments that are internal (across the top) and external (across the bottom). The vertical axis represents the positive dimensions (on the left side) and the negative dimensions (on the right side).

Ask these questions to fill out each category:

STRENGTHS: What organizational strengths exist that we can use to meet future challenges?

WEAKNESSES: What organizational weaknesses exist that can impede us from meeting future challenges?

OPPORTUNITIES: What opportunities exist in external factors that we could take advantage of to meet future challenges?

THREATS: What threats exist in external factors that could impede us from meeting future challenges?

SECTION II SUMMARY

We have walked through the importance of processes, people, and planning. As you now know, all three are required to have a properly formed business. The processes are critical to being able to systematize the business and keep it running to meet the mission. The people are also critical, as they formulate and run the processes. In addition, they lead the planning activities, which align efforts toward the overall vision.

The key to making all of this come together is the culture and leadership of the organization. The culture is the personality of the organization, and the leadership sets the tone for the desired culture.

SECTION III:
LASTING FREEDOM

KEY COMPONENTS

Chapter 8

THE GREAT DIFFERENTIATOR

When speaking to business owners across the country, I have found that one common theme resonates with individuals in these leadership roles: they want to better their business by improving efficiencies, cost structures, quality, and profits. They want to improve their company's turnover, employee engagement, and the overall working environment. They want to boost customer satisfaction, revenue, and sales. The best way to do this from a sustainable standpoint is through the business culture. The backbone of culture transformation is values, systems, and processes.

What is culture? The best definitions of a business culture are simple: it is an attitude of the business. It is the feeling someone experiences when he or she works in or with the business. It is the sum of the actions the people in the business consistently exhibit. It is the behaviors of the organization. Culture is the greatest differentiator between your business and the competition. The culture of a business is supported by the values of the business. It may or may not be the values placed on the walls or in the employee handbook, but it certainly is the genuine, deep-seated values of the business. The values are the guiding principles of the business. They are how you act on a regular basis, especially when faced with tough and often competing decisions. Values are the filters used for decision-making. These values support the systems and processes of the business along with each decision that is made.

"Culture eats strategy for breakfast."

—Peter Drucker, Austrian-born American management guru

How does a business owner or leader establish a culture of continuous improvement? The first step is to establish the company values. You and key members of your leadership team must be intentional in identifying, communicating, and exhibiting the values of your business. If this isn't done, the values will be set with or without leadership's involvement. Every time a behavior strays from the desired values and is not corrected, a new value is being set, and this one may not be desirable. Every business has values, and if positive values are clearly defined, understood, and followed, they can lead to a positive culture.

Culture is ultimately the feeling you get from an organization, whether as a visitor, an employee, or a customer. It's that sense you get about a place. Culture is created by the organization's leaders, whom we will identify later. The values of an organization are the foundation of its culture. Eventually, the behaviors and actions of an organization that are repeated and tolerated—or even encouraged—become the culture that affects others, internally and externally. The culture of the organization is critical because it is the personality of the business that all experience.

Culture is the greatest differentiator of all aspects of the organization. All other things being equal, culture has the strongest impact on the direction and success of an organization. Success, in this case, is defined as meeting the mission of the organization. Culture trumps all other focal points. Some claim that competitive advantage, strategy, and the like are just as important as culture. It is hard to argue with this, but it must be said that at some point, the importance of culture, whether positive or negative, will have to be realized for these areas to have the impact they should.

There have been financially successful organizations with less-than-desirable cultures. I have personally worked for some of these companies along my career path. It is obvious that while the cultures were not particularly desirable, they did promote success to some degree. Had these companies worked on their cultures with intentionality and open minds, their success would have been even greater financially and from other successful standpoints, as there are many definitions of success. One of these companies regularly loses its "A" players, for example. This regular churn of hiring, training, losing, and rehiring is a very costly endeavor. Not only does it cost them the direct dollars on the P&L from the expenses associated with the recruiting process; it also costs them soft dollars, which, by the way, are not really *soft*. These soft dollars are most likely the costliest, as the company suffers the loss of experience, momentum, team dynamics, and energy.

When a group that has formed into a dynamic high-performance team loses a team member, the process of reforming the team must begin again with the new team member. Trust suffers for a period of time, the learning curve must be scaled by the new member, and relationships must be reconstructed within a new dynamic. This costs more energy and time than any amount of recruiting dollars can account for in the profit column. If the loss results in an undesirable culture, the impact is even greater. The tribal knowledge goes out the door, the engagement of those who remain is affected, and work suffers.

So why do organizations fail to address culture openly and with the resources available to them? There are several reasons for this: (1) they don't know how to do this; (2) they do not have the skill set to do this; and (3) they misunderstand the term *soft skills*, believing it means "soft impact." Many times, as companies grow and scale, they are so focused on sales and revenue that the infrastructure and foundation of the business suffer attention. Eventually, the company stalls in growth as the people and processes demand attention. A company cannot grow past the capable structure it has built to sustain the increased demands, and it will not grow past the capabilities of the leaders within its walls.

TYPE OF CULTURE

To be intentional about a culture for your business, you will first have to describe the culture you are building. Go back to the core values, because they are the bedrock of the culture. Take some time to write what you see and feel from the culture once it fulfills the view you have for the organization.

The type of culture we recommend is a high-performance, transparent one. A high-performance culture allows for room to grow, the ability to delegate, and a clear path to making your vision story a reality. Transparency supports an open and communicative environment in which mistakes are allowed so learning can lead to better results.

A leader of a high-performing, transparent culture will strive not to make the fundamental attribution error. The fundamental attribution error is best described in the following way: when we act in response to a situation, we deem our intent good, even though when witnessing another's actions in the same situation, we judge that individual as having made the wrong choice. In other words, we don't give others the same grace we give ourselves. In a high-performing organization, colleagues have overcome this, for the most part, and give one another the benefit of the doubt.

> *"Profit and growth come from customers that can boast about your product or service."*

—W. Edwards Deming, American consultant

ONE IS NOT LIKE THE OTHER

In the end, between two companies being equal in everything other than their culture, the company with the high-performing culture will have a competitive advantage. For example, take store A versus store B. They can have the same storefront, the same merchandise, people with the same skill level, and the same prices. Yet, when the cultures are different, the results will be different.

Let's say store A has a culture of precision and legalism. They do everything by the book. They follow strict policies and procedures. Most decisions run through the store manager, who is also the owner. She is a nice woman; however, she demands things be done a certain way: *her* way.

Store B has a culture of high performance. They have standard operating procedures and are trained in them. They have policies, but they like to call them *guidelines*. They speak daily about core values and the company's mission. The owner is not the store manager, as she has delegated that duty to one of her long-term employees.

You can likely see the difference already. Store A doesn't have a poor culture; it just doesn't have a great culture. Store B has a culture that has provided freedom to the owner by teaching the team to be able to handle company decisions. While the two stores appear similar, on closer inspection, by way of shopping, we will see the dramatic difference.

As a customer experiences store A, he or she realizes the staff is particular about certain things. They have a strict return policy with little regard of the impact on the customer. When questions are asked about merchandise, the staff members are polite but seem to be preoccupied with the tasks they are undertaking. Instead of putting the client first, they are worried about restocking the shelves and doing paperwork, in the name of efficiency. For many decisions, the owner has to be asked before staff members can provide answers to customers.

At store B, the customer is greeted with a smile and a friendly hello. The staff members know their focus is on taking care of the customer. The return policy does have a process; however, each staff member knows he or she will be supported in doing what it takes to serve the customer. In fact, one of their core values is "wow the customer." The manager has instructed the team on how to make decisions on their own in most situations. When mistakes are made, it is considered a learning experience for the staff members and the manager. They share the responsibility to continuously improve.

Which store do you want to own? I know you said B. It's obvious that having the right culture can result in not only time freedom for the owner but also in money freedom. As the culture is felt and experienced by the customer, revenue and profits increase. The culture of the organization is the great differentiator from one competitor to another. In fact, I have seen companies that work on nothing but turning around the culture go from the red to the black on their income statement. The reason is so simple yet profound. They light a fire under the people and processes by aligning the organization to fulfill their purpose. They take away the barriers to success.

"Culture is the best strategy."

—**Gregory Gray, founder and CEO of Gray Solutions, LLC**

LEADERFLUENCE

Leadership is the ultimate answer to building and maintaining a high-performance culture. Without leaders applying true leadership, the values, systems, and processes will not be effective. The leaders of the organization must set the tone and expectations for the culture that is desired in a business.

Proper leadership is best defined as "influence." Anyone in the position to influence another person is in a position of leadership. It is not a position of authority, a title, or a right. It must be given by those who follow and earned by those who desire to lead. Some of the most influential leaders I have seen in my career are those who are not necessarily in the classic job role of a leader, but they've served as leaders within their teams because of their integrity and sense of purpose. Of course, I have also seen incredible leaders in positions of authority. Regardless of the position they hold, these extraordinary leaders influence others through their opinions, actions, and involvement within the business. They lead and influence others in a way the others want to follow. They exhibit what we have termed *leaderfluence*.

What makes some people such strong leaders? First, they are persistently pursuing a cause. They speak and act with passion and emotion for a specific motive. They have a vision that they share with others as they elicit others' buy-in to that vision. It could be as simple as supporting the company vision, mission, values, and processes completely and intending to uphold them. Or it could be that they are seeking some radical change. Regardless, they pursue the cause with fervor and unwavering consistency.

Second, they genuinely care for those with whom they work. Sure, we have all seen some in leadership positions strive for results while seemingly failing to care about the individuals involved; however, that is not sustainable. They lose either momentum or their people—or both. Real leaders show they care for those around them regardless of whether it benefits their cause. The people who are attracted to following their lead can do so from a place of trust because they know their interests matter.

Third, a leader exhibits integrity and transparency. A leader of a high-performance team holds him- or herself as accountable to the vision or cause as anyone else. They are capable of being vulnerable, and admit their own faults and shortcomings along the journey. These leaders are clear in their expectations and communication to others, no matter where they fit within the hierarchy of the organization. Again, they build trust, as they are seen as honest and forthright.

> *"Leadership is the ability to get people to do what they don't want to do and like it."*
>
> **—President Harry S. Truman**

CULTURE ON DISPLAY

An organization's leaders set its cultural expectations. However, it is the collective people of the organization—who fulfill the work and satisfy the customers' needs—who ultimately determine the culture of the company. How these individuals interact with customers, other organizations, and one another is the culture that is seen and felt.

Choices and behaviors that are repeatedly allowed to occur become the culture. To keep the culture from shifting to something undesirable, it must be protected at all costs. This means that when a behavior is demonstrated outside of what is desirable, it must be addressed immediately. When a culture is deeply ingrained, many times these corrections will take place without a leader having to engage with an employee. We have evidence that when employees correct other employees, the culture expectations are being clearly understood and are working as they should be. This is authentic, influential leadership being exhibited.

When setting culture expectations, the company values, policies, and standard operating procedures are a great place to start. These should clearly articulate the vision of the desired culture. As performance appraisals are given to employees, they should tie back to the expectations originally given in these areas. As the saying goes, "What gets measured gets managed." This is true in behaviors as well. The key is to make the desired culture so important that it is top of mind for everyone in the organization. In regular communications and meetings, the company values should be stated and restated.

One of the most significant areas in which company culture is affected is in hiring practices. Many small businesses struggle with finding quality people to fulfill roles. When faced with hiring for a position, the question often arises whether to hire for skills or attitude. The short-term answer is hire for skill. The long-term answer is hire for attitude. The best scenario is to hire for both. The person with specific skills can seem like the best answer, especially when work is backed up and needs to be processed. However, the more important question is, "Does this individual fit the culture I desire for my business?" If you cannot answer that in the affirmative, then that person does not belong in the organization, regardless of his or her skill set. The culture is too important to settle for anything less than a proper fit.

The key is to attract people into the organization who are engaged and willing to support the values, systems, and processes. Should you find that current members of the organization are not doing these things, then it is time for a change. Sure, you will potentially miss their skills in the short term; however, as you train others, the overall culture of the organization will improve. It is much more effective to train for skills than to accept inappropriate attitudes and lack of engagement. This affects overall performance in the areas of quality, efficiency, customer satisfaction, and profitability. It also affects the morale of the employees who do honor the culture expectations.

In the end, it is your decision as a business owner to take appropriate actions. If you truly want a culture of high performance being conveyed to everyone who touches your business, then you will do the work required to make that happen. It is up to you and the leaders within your organization to set clear expectations and let others know when their behaviors are out of bounds. Find or attract leaders within your organization who can assist you in building this culture of high performance. You may currently have some individuals on staff who would enjoy stepping up and influencing others, as they know they have your support. If not, then start recruiting them now. Remember, leaders are the influencers within all departments of the company.

Chapter 9

ON YOUR MARK, GET SET, GO!

Our advice and your knowledge thus far about transforming your business to one of freedom is only as beneficial as the actions you take. Knowledge is good, but applied knowledge is better. You must take the knowledge, apply it, make mistakes fast, correct them through a continuous-improvement mind-set, and eventually succeed. There are three key action processes that will supercharge your business if done correctly and consistently.

MEETINGS

The most misunderstood tool from small businesses all the way to large corporations is meetings. Meetings can be a colossal waste of time or extremely powerful. I have been a part of both and have led both. I learned through my own and others' mistakes and have dialed in a very practical and effective way for small businesses to determine what types of meetings are necessary. I have seen these meetings in action over many years, and they work very well.

There are four types of meetings that a small business should have as part of the normal routine. In some cases, these can be adjusted for a specific industry or business type. Again, consistency and focus are needed for these to be efficient and effective.

1. Owner meetings

2. Leadership meetings

3. System meetings

4. All-team meetings

The owner meeting is required for the owner(s) and the CEO (most likely an owner). They meet to review the vision, discuss the strategic plan, and discuss financial results. They also review KPIs of the overall business. This is a quick meeting—less than an hour in duration—held on a monthly basis, if not more frequently. If there is one owner, then he or she should set this time aside to review the information indicated above and take some time to reflect on the business. If the business is a one-owner business, we highly suggest that the owner have a business coach or be a part of a mastermind team who can discuss these items with the owner.

The leadership meeting is likely the most important meeting for a small business. This is where the strategic direction and the tactical actions mesh. This meeting is made up of the CEO (usually an owner) and the leader of each business system (finance, sales, operations, etc.). We recommend that this meeting be held weekly, at a minimum. The duration should be no more than two hours. An hour is better if you can cover all agenda items during that time. It is best to keep this meeting moving by redirecting long-winded topics to a later time for further discussion. The key is to cover all KPIs and big rocks (priorities).

The system meetings are the functional-areas meetings led by the team leader of each business system. These are much more tactics-based meetings, with KPIs and weekly actions being the basis of what is covered. These meeting should occur at least once a week; however, some departments (such as operations) benefit from quick daily stand-up meetings. If held on a weekly basis, then these may last up to an hour. If they are going longer, then something likely needs adjusting. If you are meeting daily, I would attempt to limit them to fifteen minutes. The key is to share information, such as the KPIs, beforehand so the meeting is congratulating exceptional results and focusing on the exceptions that need improvement. Individuals in all roles that report to the system leader should attend.

All-team meetings are to be held twice a year. These are all-employee meetings for building rapport, sharing information, and imparting a general status of the business. We recommend that a financial overview with what's appropriate to share with all employees, a results overview (KPIs), and rewards be covered at this time. It is a good idea to always discuss the vision, mission, and values in these meetings, as these are the baseline of the culture expectations. Handing out recognition awards to employees in front of their peers is important to the team; it builds momentum and trust. Have fun with these meetings. Buy the attendees lunch and have an entertaining contest of some sort. Show the team that leadership and the employees are united in their efforts.

Some requirements for purposeful and time-worthy meetings are an agenda; meeting minutes; and a vision, mission, and values review. Before every meeting, an agenda must be sent to team members. It is fine for a standing agenda to be used; however, a fluid one is better if the items might change. The first things to be covered on the agenda are the company's vision, mission, and values. These are the cornerstone of the culture you are building and must always be front and center. Once the meeting is complete, the meeting minutes should be sent to all attendees. This is critical, as what is heard can be interpreted differently by the attendees. The key is to memorialize the meeting for future reference as well as allow each person to review and adjust to what was discussed or speak up if they heard something differently. Do not skip this step, or you will lose out on one of the most powerful intentions of meetings.

ACTION PLANS

Many books have been written on taking action, prioritizing, and maximizing productivity. Over the years, we have learned that simple is better. Many elaborate software programs, planning tricks, and productivity tools have been created, and some are even good. However, what we have seen is that nothing beats plain old organization and follow-up.

While we have been coaching and teaching these principles for many years, we were pleased to discover a to-the-point book that covers much of what we believe to be true and effective. If you are interested in reading a book in which some of these principles are outlined, then spend some time in *The 12 Week Year*, by Brian P. Moran and Michael Lennington. In this book, the authors cover prioritization and periodization. We strongly believe that these are true secrets to effectively taking action, and we have seen them create positive results within businesses.

Throughout this book, I have referred to priorities as *big rocks*. I attribute my use of this term to Stephen Covey, as it is from him that I first heard it. I will paraphrase the story for you with some added perspective. I have found that the results are powerful and real if you focus in the way that this scenario reveals you should.

There are two buckets on a table, along with three big rocks and a pail of pebbles. I pour the pebbles into the bucket. This leaves about 20 percent of the bucket space remaining. I now tell you to add the three big rocks without allowing anything to breach the edge of the bucket. No matter how you try to fit in all three rocks, the third rock will just not fit. You can press into the pebbles all you want, but they only move so far. So you leave out a big rock.

With the second bucket, I instruct you to use your own creativity and judgment. You decide to place the big rocks in first. Then you pour the pebbles on top of them. While not all the pebbles fit, most do, but all the big rocks made it in first. So we pick up the few pebbles that fell to the side. It is a small number with regard to the total number of pebbles.

So what did we observe? Let's take a closer look at what the big rocks represent. They are the priorities you have in place for the next twelve weeks. They are the things that will move the dial for your business. You can have many more big rocks in your life; however, I want to keep this concept simple for now and focused closely on your business.

In this scenario, what do the pebbles represent? They are the day-to-day important and pressing items but not the priorities. They are things that will take you away from your priorities if you let them. They will assist you in saying things like, "We work hard all day every day, but we don't seem to be making progress," or "I am working long hours. How can I possibly add any time to my schedule to work on the big rocks and priorities?" This is normal. When one is in a reactive environment instead of a proactive culture, this is the norm.

So what happens to the pebbles that don't fit in the bucket? They are handled in a few different ways. First, they can be delegated. Have someone handle them so you can focus on the priorities. Second, and a better solution, is to work on processes and systems so these pebbles are reduced through efficiency and effectiveness. We have seen this be very successful. Third, and least effective, is to let them fall where they may. While that may be good for the short term, especially as processes are being improved, ignoring these pebbles could result in them becoming a priority. You don't want that to happen.

We prescribe and have seen the best gains in priority completion by periodization. As you can guess by the title, the book we referenced above suggests a twelve-week time frame. Whether you use eight weeks, ten weeks, or twelve weeks is not important, as long as you choose an appropriate short term that forces careful planning and focus to get things accomplished. Since twelve weeks is roughly equivalent to a fiscal quarter, this resonates with most of our clients. I personally prefer ten weeks, as it allows me to fit five quarters of work into one year. This has been a powerful mental technique for some of our clients.

Regardless of the time frame, the methodology works. When we set goals for longer time frames, things tend to lag. As business owners, we need to keep ourselves focused and intentionally push ourselves and our teams to accomplish what is important. You must have a strong desire deep within you to accomplish these things. You need the energy and drive to make this happen, as it is not human nature. Our nature is to handle the obvious instead of driving the priorities to the forefront. If we miss a day or week in our priority plans, nothing bad happens—at least not right away. Nobody yells, no severe consequences arise that day, nor do we feel bad about it until later. Now you know it is not a good thing. You have been made aware.

12-WEEK FOCUS

NAME OF RESPONSIBLE PARTY: _____

12-WEEK GOALS		
FOR THE TERM ENDING _____(MONTH)_____(DAY)		
GOAL 1:		
TACTICS	WEEK DUE	STATUS
GOAL 2:		
TACTICS	WEEK DUE	STATUS
GOAL 3:		
TACTICS	WEEK DUE	STATUS

Let's use exercise as an example. While I exercise five days a week, I don't necessarily like to spend time exercising. There are so many other things I would love to do. However, due to my life vision, exercise is a priority. Now, I will admit that from time to time, I like it, but what I really enjoy are the effects of exercise. The priority is now a habit because I have done it for so long. What if I didn't exercise? Missing a day or so occasionally wouldn't knock me off the path of keeping this as a priority. However, if I am to achieve my overarching life goal of being healthy, then regular exercise is a requirement.

A few years ago, I experienced an injury that kept me from exercising for over a year, at least to the level at which I was used to performing. For months, I couldn't exercise at all. I injured my Achilles tendon. Walking without pain was a challenge, and things like running and cycling were out of the question. The only thing that kept me focused on and engaged in getting back to exercising was my priority to do so. This was a true test of my commitment because I could have easily let the task of exercise go altogether as I found other things to fill my time. I truly lost the habit but never the priority goal. Happily, I can attest to the fact that I did heal and am now back to meeting my expectations in this area.

If you set a goal to exercise but then skip days regularly, guess what? This becomes your new habit. Skipping days becomes accepted by you subconsciously, if not consciously. When this happens, you will not meet your priority goal. This holds true in business as well. If you allow your priorities to go unmonitored, they will slip, and eventually you will not do what you intended to do in your business. Remember, your priority items are the most important, as they move the dial on your company. You must stay the course with them to truly find freedom in your business.

Chapter 10
SHOW ME THE MONEY

There are two key areas every business owner should be competent in: sales and finance. This doesn't mean you have to do all the work in these areas. It does mean that you must have a handle on the inter-working of these systems, however.

Sales and marketing are the lifeblood of a business because these systems attract customers, build growth, and ensure revenue is generated. Without revenue, nothing else matters. You must under-stand the metrics you are using and monitor them as part of your normal course of action.

Determine an appropriate period of time between reviewing the metrics. We recommend that sales and marketing KPIs are reviewed weekly, at a minimum. Depending on your type of business, you may want to go over them more often.

Sales and marketing are two distinctly different disciplines. Whether they are managed within the same system or functional department, or separately, depends on the size of your business, the complexity of your business model, and your goals.

Marketing consists of the activities that soften the market for the selling activity. It is about building a brand, creating a story, and identifying the ideal client. Marketing also occurs in the daily interactions of your team as they exhibit your culture to your clients.

Sales includes the activities of taking orders, receiving payments, and fulfilling orders. The system for sales may be different from one product or service to another.

ATTRACT AND REPEL

It is important that your marketing activities attract the ideal clients for your business. It is equally important to detract those with whom you would prefer not to do business. Do not fall into the trap of promoting to a wider audience than you need to. The power of marketing is in the specificity of the niche to which you are speaking.

Determine the exact market to which you want to sell. Be very specific in describing the ideal customer. Even in business-to-business sales, this is critical. Time wasted in fielding calls or following up on leads that aren't in your target audience consumes energy and resources from your business.

Every activity you do within your business can be considered part of your brand and is therefore part of your marketing. As your team members interact with customers or prospective customers through the various customer-facing functions, they are showcasing your culture and your brand. This may be as powerful—or even more powerful—than any advertisement you run.

Create an intentional marketing plan each year. This should be part of your strategic-plan discussions. Outlining whether you are expanding into new markets or doubling down on ones you are selling to now is an important part of the strategy going forward.

The sales system is critical to the overall success of a business. Once marketing has done the job of attracting new customers or getting the attention of current customers, the sales process must close the deals. Without continued growth and/or solid repeat customers, the business's longevity will suffer.

As with all processes, the sales process should be measured and reviewed regularly. By having specific KPIs for sales activities and results, it is easy for a business owner to proactively watch the sales pipeline. This is critical, as it assists in predicting production, inventory, and capacity needs from an operational standpoint. It also gives the business owner, sales manager, and the sales team clear data on what is working and not working from a sales and marketing standpoint. It allows your team members to adjust their activities to support the KPI goals.

EXAMPLE KPIS FOR SALES AND MARKETING ACTIVITIES

CATEGORY	MEASURE	STATUS
LEADS	NUMBER OF LEADS PER WEEK	NUMBER TO GOAL
PROSPECTS	NUMBER OF LEADS CONVERTED TO PROSPECTS	PERCENT CONVERTED TO GOAL
SALES	NUMBER OF PROSPECTS SOLD	PERCENT SOLD TO GOAL
AD SPEND	COST PER LEAD	OVER/UNDER GOAL
AD SPEND	COST PER SALE	OVER/UNDER GOAL

Have these measures given to you weekly if not daily so you, as the business owner, can understand whether your business is growing or shrinking based on the leading indicators and not the trailing indicators that come from financial statements.

FOLLOW THE MONEY

The finance and accounting systems of a business may seem less than exciting to a business owner, yet they are critical to understand. The owner must fully grasp the basic reports and tools used to review financial performance and plan for the business. While we do recommend you delegate the work surrounding finance and accounting, you need to maintain a close relationship with this team and conduct regular reviews.

BASIC REPORTS AND INFORMATION

1. P&L statement: This is often called the *income statement*. It summarizes the revenue, costs, and income of the business and should be reviewed monthly.

2. Balance sheet: This is a snapshot view of the state of the business. It shows the business's assets and liabilities as well as the equity of the owners.

3. Cash flow statement: Simply put, this summarizes the inflow and outflow of cash for a business at any given time. It bridges the income statement and the balance sheet.

4. Line of credit: This is the credit extended to your business from your bank.

5. Bank accounts: These are the different accounts set up to withdraw from or deposit money into your bank.

6. Accounts receivable: This is the revenue promised the business but not yet collected. It is an asset.

7. Accounts payable: This is monies owed to creditors, suppliers, and/or vendors. It is a liability.

COMMON FINANCIAL MEASURES AND RATIOS

1. Gross profit margin: This measures operational efficiency and pricing strategy.

$$\frac{\text{SALES—COST OF GOODS SOLD} \times 100}{\text{SALES}}$$

2. Net profit margin: This measures efficiency after all expenses.

$$\frac{\text{NET PROFIT AFTER TAX} \times 100}{\text{SALES}}$$

3. Return on assets: This measures the efficient use of assets.

$$\frac{\text{NET PROFIT AFTER TAX} \times 100}{\text{TOTAL ASSETS}}$$

4. Current ratio: This measures the ability to pay short-term debt.

$$\frac{\text{CURRENT ASSETS}}{\text{CURRENT LIABILITIES}}$$

5. Quick ratio: This measures short-term liquidity.

$$\frac{\text{CURRENT ASSETS—INVENTORIES}}{\text{CURRENT LIABILITIES}}$$

6. Debt ratio: This measures the risk or leverage of the business.

$$\frac{\text{TOTAL LIABILITIES}}{\text{TOTAL ASSETS}}$$

7. Asset ratio: This measures the efficient use of the assets. It is also called *asset turnover*.

$$\frac{\text{SALES}}{\text{TOTAL ASSETS}}$$

8. Average collection period—This measures the effectiveness of the collection process.

$$\frac{\text{RECEIVABLES} \times 365 \text{ DAYS}}{\text{ANNUAL CREDIT SALES}}$$

9. Inventory turnover: This measures the efficient use of inventory investment.

$$\frac{\text{COST OF GOODS SOLD}}{\text{AVERAGE INVENTORY}}$$

WITHOUT CASH, IT DIES

As the old saying "cash is king" implies, without cash, everything else stops or dies. If you ever find your business in a cash deficit situation, you will understand. It is a vital need for a business owner to understand the cash flow of the business.

"But my business is profitable!" says the owner who is missing payroll for the first time. I have heard this many times in working with business owners. I had a business owner call me one time and show me his P&L statement with over a hundred thousand dollars on the bottom line. His question was, "Where is it? It certainly isn't in my bank account." As troubling as this can seem, it is all too real. Actual cash on hand and profits are two different things.

There are many reasons behind this. A few of the common issues include the following:

1. Accounting methods—accrual vs. cash basis

2. Terms on payables and receivables

3. Timing of transactions

4. Inventory

The key is understanding that while profitable, you may still be in a cash deficit. This is really important, especially for new business owners, to understand. You must know what your cash status is at any given moment.

HOW TO INCREASE CASH

If you find your business cash position lacking, there are several things discussed in this chapter that can have a positive impact.

1. Extend payable timing—through business credit cards and other means

2. Increase your pricing

3. Speed up your receivables through terms and other methods

4. Research leasing vs. owning

5. Consider lines of credit

The bottom line here is to focus on increasing your cash on hand and your cash flow. It will help you sleep better at night and ensure your business can continue on its mission.

A SIMPLE WAY TO MANAGE DAY-TO-DAY RESPONSIBILITIES

We teach business owners a simple way to manage the day-to-day responsibilities of their businesses without having to look at financial and cash flow reports. We teach the system put forth in Mike Michalowicz's book *Profit First*. The basic premise is to set up multiple bank accounts for your business. These accounts can be referred to as *buckets* for holding cash to be used for different applications.

THE FIVE CORE ACCOUNTS WE HAVE SET UP FOR OUR BUSINESS ARE AS FOLLOWS:

1. **MAIN:** This is where we pay for all our operational expenses.

2. **INCOME:** This is where all revenue comes into our business.

3. **TAX:** This is the account where we hold tax dollars to be paid out quarterly and yearly.

4. **PROFIT:** This is the account where profits are accumulated.

5. **OWNER COMP:** This is the account that pays me, the business owner.

THE FOLLOWING ARE SOME ADDITIONAL ACCOUNTS WE RECOMMEND:

1. **GIVING:** This is the account where we accumulate donations for charity.

2. **BONUS:** This is the account where we accumulate bonuses for employees and contractors.

Of course, you may have other accounts you want to add for your specific business or industry. The point is to use the accounts to proactively stay on top of your business. Relying on financial statements to look forward is like looking in the rearview mirror and driving backward; it just doesn't make sense.

The key to using the accounts is knowing the percentages to place in each. It will take some calculations to determine the correct amounts; however, it isn't difficult to do. Work with your CPA and bookkeeper to devise a plan. You can adjust as you learn more along the way. If you don't know where to begin, we suggest starting at 1 percent for the profit account. Looking at the historical data on your financial statements should give you a good indication of how to get started.

IN SUMMARY

Marketing and finance can be two of the most confusing and misunderstood aspects of the business to the business owner. We suggest that you find someone to advise you and teach you these aspects of the business, as well as guide you through the decisions you will need to make. There are experts available who can explain the steps you need to take for your specific business.

For marketing guidance, there are firms that can do all of the work or just portions of the work, or they can give you guidance to do the work yourself. I recommend that unless you have performed the work before, you hire someone to take care of the details for you. With today's climate of rapid change in social media and marketing preferences, it's a lot to keep up with when you are running a business full time. Find an adviser and competent firm to do that hard work for you.

When it comes to finance, you need to be proficient at reading and understanding your company's financial reports. Your CPA may offer some guidance, but they are typically more versed in the tax implications and accounting standards. Understanding business finance and being able to make projection-based decisions requires a different set of skills. Finance strategy takes more of a proactive mind-set. When we engage with our clients, we help them create budgets and pro formas for looking into the future. Don't sell yourself short by abdicating the responsibility to other professionals.

CONCLUSION

Don't let the amount of information we have discussed dissuade you from doing the work. Just start with the life plan and the vision story. Take one step at a time and work through the chapters. If you need help, reach out to us. We have mastermind groups, coaching engagements, and online courses to help you find your way to freedom.

We have witnessed hundreds of business owners take these steps and experience drastic transformation. We have seen small businesses change in less than a year from accepting chaos as normal to freeing themselves from chaos and overwhelm. You can always count on chaos to be lurking in or near your business; however, it can be dealt with as processes, people, and planning are put in their proper places.

The crown jewel of your business will be the high-performance culture that results from proper leadership and effective vision, mission, and values being understood and upheld in every decision. The culture of your business will be the personality of your business that all employees, vendors, and customers will experience. It will be your brand that sets the course for what you promise to your customers. Your culture will be the great differentiator between you and your competition.

Give it all you have from an implementation standpoint, and the results will be fantastic. Set aside ego and pride, and get the work done. If your mission is truly worthy, you will do whatever it takes to make it come to light. Stay on the course to the vision you see and persevere through the trials and tribulations that will arise. Success is not in the destination but, rather, in the journey you take. I wish you all the best and pray for each and every person who has read these pages.

Enjoy the journey!

APPENDIX

TOOLS AND RESOURCES

The following are books for the business owner. We referenced some of them in this book, and we recommend the others as additional resources. They are organized by general subject matter.

MIND-SET AND YOU

- *The Big Leap*, by Gay Hendricks
- *48 Days to the Work You Love*, by Dan Miller
- *Living Forward*, by Michael Hyatt and Daniel Harkavy
- *Think and Grow Rich*, by Napoleon Hill
- *StrengthsFinder 2.0*, by Tom Rath
- *The Road Back to You*, by Ian Morgan Cron and Suzanne Stabile
- *See You at the Top*, by Zig Ziglar

LEADERSHIP AND ACCOUNTABILITY

- *QBQ!*, by John G. Miller
- *The 17 Indisputable Laws of Teamwork*, by John C. Maxwell
- *The Five Dysfunctions of a Team*, by Patrick Lencioni
- *Leadership and the One Minute Manager*, by Ken Blanchard, Patricia Zigarmi, and Drea Zigarmi

- *The 12 Week Year,* by Brian P. Moran and Michael Lennington
- *Rocket Fuel,* by Gino Wickman and Mark C. Winters
- *The Dream Manager,* by Matthew Kelly
- *The Fred Factor,* by Mark Sanborn

SMALL-BUSINESS SYSTEMS AND PROCESSES

- *The E-Myth Revisited,* by Michael E. Gerber
- *The Lifestyle Business Owner,* by Aaron Muller
- *Mastering the Rockefeller Habits,* by Verne Harnish
- *The Goal,* by Eliyahu M. Goldratt and Jeff Cox

FINANCES

- *Profit First,* by Mike Michalowicz
- *Rich Dad's Cashflow Quadrant,* by Robert T. Kiyosaki

STRATEGY AND PLANNING

- *Foundations in Strategic Management,* by Jeffrey S. Harrison and Caron H. St. John

ONLINE LINKS

- Business Owner Freedom Podcast and Blog, https://www.businessownerfreedom.com/blog
- Business Owner Freedom Mastermind, https://www.businessownerfreedom.com/mastermind
- DiSC assessments, contact us at info@gregorygray.com
- LegalShield, https://gregoryhgray.wearelegalshield.com/

- Free Vision Story Quick Course (use the code "Book" to get the 100 percent discount), https://www.businessownerfreedom.com/visionstory

- Free Four Steps to Business Freedom Masterclass, https://www.businessownerfreedom.com/FreeVirtualTraining

- Gray University: We provide courses, worksheets, forms, templates, and weekly discussion points for you and your team, as well as ongoing education for implementation, https://www.gray.university

ABOUT THE AUTHOR

GREGORY GRAY

Gregory Gray, owner of Gray Solutions LLC and co-owner of Pro Coach Company, left the corporate world in 2010 to pursue his vision story. Along the way he has bought, sold, and currently owns several businesses. He helps businesses develop dynamic leaders and teams supported by high-performance cultures. He also guides them through transformation of their systems and processes. Through his teaching and coaching, he is transforming businesses and lives.

As an executive coach and business advisor, Gregory will help you find freedom in your business and life. Gray Solutions LLC offers courses, programs, and workshops specifically designed to effect positive transformation so you can realize your desired vision and lifestyle. He is also the host of the Business Owner Freedom Podcast, which explores subjects for small business owners weekly.

Gregory is the father of two daughters and has been married for over two decades to his best friend, Kim. They live south of Nashville on a farm where they raise grass-fed beef and lamb. They also enjoy riding their horses and playing with their retrievers. They love their lifestyle and are living their vision daily.

OUR SERVICES

GRAY SOLUTIONS, LLC PROVIDES:

BUSINESS AND LIFE COACHING:

www.GREGORYGRAY.com

BUSINESS OWNER FREEDOM PODCAST:

www.BUSINESSOWNERFREEDOM.com

BUSINESS RESOURCES
CONNECTION. EDUCATION. IMPLEMENTATION:

www.GRAY.university

Printed in the USA
CPSIA information can be obtained
at www.ICGtesting.com
JSHW012030140824
68134JS00033B/2977

9 781599 324807